THE 3 GAPS

THE 3 GAPS

Are You Making a Difference?

Hyrum W. Smith

Berrett–Koehler Publishers, Inc.
San Francisco
a BK Life book

Berrett-Koehler Publishers, Inc.
1333 Broadway, Suite 1000
Oakland, CA 94612-1921
Tel: (510) 817-2277   Fax: (510) 817-2278   www.bkconnection.com

Ordering Information

Quantity sales. Special discounts are available on quantity purchases by corporations, associations, and others. For details, contact the "Special Sales Department" at the Berrett-Koehler address above.
Individual sales. Berrett-Koehler publications are available through most bookstores. They can also be ordered directly from Berrett-Koehler: Tel: (800) 929-2929; Fax: (802) 864-7626; www.bkconnection.com
Orders for college textbook/course adoption use. Please contact Berrett-Koehler: Tel: (800) 929-2929; Fax: (802) 864-7626.
Orders by U.S. trade bookstores and wholesalers. Please contact Ingram Publisher Services, Tel: (800) 509-4887; Fax: (800) 838-1149; E-mail: customer .service@ingrampublisherservices.com; or visit www.ingrampublisherservices .com/Ordering for details about electronic ordering.

Berrett-Koehler and the BK logo are registered trademarks of Berrett-Koehler Publishers, Inc.

Printed in the United States of America

Berrett-Koehler books are printed on long-lasting acid-free paper. When it is available, we choose paper that has been manufactured by environmentally responsible processes. These may include using trees grown in sustainable forests, incorporating recycled paper, minimizing chlorine in bleaching, or recycling the energy produced at the paper mill.

Library of Congress Cataloging-in-Publication Data

Names: Smith, Hyrum W., author.
Title: The 3 gaps : are you making a difference? / Hyrum W. Smith.
Other titles: Three gaps
Description: First edition. | Oakland, CA : Berrett-Koehler Publishers, [2015]
Identifiers: LCCN 2015034300 | ISBN 9781626566620 (pbk.)
Subjects: LCSH: Conduct of life. | Peace of mind. | Success.
Classification: LCC BJ1589 .S647 2015 | DDC 170/.44—dc23
LC record available at http://lccn.loc.gov/2015034300

First Edition
20 19 18 17 16 15   10 9 8 7 6 5 4 3 2 1

Cover designer: Nancy Austin

I dedicate this book
to my amazing wife of forty-nine years,
my six children, and my twenty-four grandchildren.
They have all consistently been there
to help me close
my gaps.

Contents

Foreword

In George Bernard Shaw's remarkable book *Man and Superman* the fictional hero, Don Juan, is faced with an interesting choice. He has been sent to hell and has to consider the consequences of his condition. He has been given a choice to return to heaven, but the devil is persuasively and deftly trying to get him to stay. Hell, in this instance, is described as a very nice place to be—sophisticated, pleasant, easy, and not the fire and brimstone of mythology. In the end Don Juan wisely chooses to return to heaven, a choice scoffed at by the devil, who asks why. Our hero simply answers that "to be in Hell is to drift; to be in Heaven is to steer." The devil is rendered speechless.

Hyrum Smith has long held a special interest in the principles of productivity and achievement. Hyrum has been blessed with the ability to electrify and enlarge the minds and aspirations of his audiences. His energy forges a compelling pathway to something he calls inner peace; a profound by-product of achieving congruity between what is of most worth, based on the highest priorities and acts of behavior. As he explains in the following pages, incongruity happens when we veer off the path of what matters most and lose our way. You will recognize that condition; it's a common malady in life— in his life, our lives, organizations, and, perhaps most especially, the life of our nation.

We live in a world of incongruity and confusion. Yet finding inner peace is a process that is surprisingly easy to learn and apply—the remedy for much of the chaos lies within the pages of this book. Will being influenced by the wisdom shared here and applying it in our lives change us? Can our organizations become more focused and productive? Could it heal the nation? Well, that depends. Are we ready to change ourselves? If so, the fruits of that effort will be rich.

We, like Don Juan, can choose to drift or steer through our lives. Although this is not a book that offers heaven as a reward, Hyrum extends an emphatic opportunity for us to steer ourselves in the direction where our highest ideals, great accomplishments, and the contentment that comes from being whole lie in wait. Read on. Make a difference.

Richard I. Winwood, cofounder of Franklin Covey
and Developer of the Franklin Day Planner

Introduction

I lived in England when I was nineteen and twenty years old and had the opportunity of listening to Winston Churchill speak. In a speech that he gave just before his death, he indicated that he had been obsessed with the need to make a difference on the planet.

If anyone has made a difference, Winston Churchill has. After all, he probably saved the free world during World War II. As I listened to him speak, I felt like a baton had been passed to me that day, and I decided, "You know what? I'm going to make a difference, too."

The commitment to that value has affected most of my decisions over the past fifty years. So when the office of then mayor Rudy Giuliani called me three weeks after the events of September 11, 2001, and asked if my business partner Stephen Covey and I would come to New York to lead a workshop for the families affected by the tragedy, I said, "Of course, when do you need us?"

On October 18, 2001, Stephen and I flew to New York. I'd flown into New York hundreds of times, but this time flying over the East River was a very different experience. The World Trade Center was gone. We flew in late at night and from our window we could only see lights and the smoke that smoldered on. It was a surreal sight.

The next morning at 5:00 a.m., a police van picked us up and took us to Ground Zero, where a tour had been arranged for us by the mayor. After getting through four police checkpoints, we stood on fifteen feet of compacted debris in front of the largest hole I'd ever seen.

As we stood there, a crane pulled an I-beam out of the rubble; it was dripping molten steel on one end. The police officer told us that there had been over forty thousand computers in the World Trade Center and not one had survived the three-thousand-degree fire. It was still burning as we stood there.

Later we were shown into a hotel ballroom designed for a capacity of eighteen hundred people. Four or five hundred additional people stood in every available space. The event began with two police officers and two firefighters in dress uniforms walking in with the American flag. Just that was enough to wipe me out emotionally. The Harlem Girls Choir then blew the roof off, singing three patriotic songs; I have never heard more magnificent music.

By then I was crying like a baby. I was grateful Stephen was up first. When it was my turn to speak, I made my way to the front of the room, stepping over people sitting on the floor. Before I could open my mouth, a firefighter stood up and said, "Mr. Smith, are you going to tell us how we're going to get out of bed in the morning when we just don't give a crap anymore?"

That began the toughest and perhaps most rewarding speaking experience I've ever had.

I looked out at the expectant, shocked, grief-stricken faces and then said to the firefighter, "If you remember one thing I say today, let it be these words: *pain is inevitable; misery is optional.* The fact is, bad things happen to good people. Wars happen. People lose their 401(k) retirement accounts. Tsunamis wipe out villages. Nuclear plants melt down. A lot of bad things happen. We're not going to get through this mortal experience without some pain. But how we choose to deal with that pain is ultimately the measure of who we are and of the success we have in closing our gaps.

"When you compare what happened here on 9/11 to what has happened on this planet in the last one hundred and fifty years, it doesn't even come up on the scope of ugliness in comparison. Does it?"

It was so quiet in that massive room you could hear a pin drop.

"Let's go back to June 5, 1944. Eisenhower is in a bunker in England and says to his generals, 'Gentlemen, we've got to throw more kids at that beach in Normandy tomorrow than the Germans have bullets in their bunkers.' The next day they threw two hundred thousand kids at that beach, and do you know what happened? The Germans ran out of bullets in their bunkers. Eisenhower had estimated within four hundred how many young men he'd lose. How often do we remember that?"

I went on to remind the audience of other tragic and monumental losses: over 400,000 soldiers lost in World

War II, more than 600,000 lost in the Civil War; we lost 50,000 soldiers in just three days at the Battle of Gettysburg. Then there was Korea. Vietnam. The list goes on.

I then said, "Let me tell you why this resonates so much with me. On May 18, 1995, my two daughters were driving home from Salt Lake City. My daughter Sharwan was twenty-four years old and three weeks away from her wedding. My daughter Stacie was twenty-five years old, and she had her two-year-old daughter with her in the car. While traveling down I-15 in Utah, they had an accident that rolled the car. Sharwan was killed instantly. My granddaughter, Shilo, was thrown from the car, killing her instantly as well. Somehow, Stacie survived.

"For the first time in my life, I experienced very deep, unbelievable pain. I had to call Sharwan's fiancé and tell him that she was dead. Stacie's husband, Larry, already knew because he had been on the phone with Stacie when the accident happened.

"Early in the morning before the funeral of my daughter and granddaughter, I sat in my office trying to come up with something to say. How do you speak at your own daughter's funeral? You never expect to outlive your kids.

"As I sat there, my eye rested on a painting in my office that has been there a very long time. It depicts a winter scene in the western prairies with a pioneer couple standing over the grave of a family member they had just buried. As I stared at the painting, I saw something I'd never noticed before. In the background there were other wagons, and people sitting on the wagons holding the reins of their horses. They were waiting for this couple to finish burying their loved one. That's when I realized what those pioneers knew, and what we all have to learn: We have to move on, or we will not survive. Those early pioneers made a difference for their future generations because they refused to quit."

Even as tears streamed down my face, I could see recognition in the faces of the audience. At that moment, they knew I understood their pain. I told them, "There are times when I still get mad as hell about losing my daughter and granddaughter, but we have to move on. That experience changed me. It forever changed my outlook on life, and I will never forget it. But if I had decided to be miserable, it would have ruined many lives, my own included."

Everyone on the planet has to deal with some pain. Regardless of that fact, misery does not have to be a part of it. If you choose misery, you're done. Your mind shuts down, and you stop thinking about the things you ought to think about, things that could build and strengthen your relationships, your body, your mind, and your business. If you choose misery, everybody around you is also miserable. The end result of misery is hopelessness.

As I looked out at the audience I realized that these people had all made a difference one way or the other in the events of 9/11. Firemen, police officers, neighbors, and bystanders: all went forward against a tide of overwhelming pain and suffering to make a difference.

I have learned that we all want to make a difference, to be significant or to make a contribution in some way so as to alleviate suffering or to make the world a better place.

This book is about making a difference, starting with you. Just as an airline flight attendant will tell you to put your own oxygen mask on before assisting others in case of cabin pressure loss, getting your own life together by learning what the Three Gaps are and how to close them will enable you to take control of yourself and your life and to make a huge difference in the world around you, both personally and professionally.

Included in each chapter discussing a gap there is a personal story. These true stories come from people I've come to know and admire over the years who have made a real difference in their own lives by closing the Three Gaps.

If you will make a commitment to internalize and act on the lessons of the Three Gaps, we guarantee that you will find new tools to live a more balanced, productive life with an increased ability to make a difference.

Closing the Gaps

Before we can talk about truly making a difference, I need to introduce an important concept. To do that, I want you to think back to 1989 and the movie *Indiana Jones and the Last Crusade*, in which the hero seeks the Holy Grail. Jones follows various clues and overcomes many obstacles to arrive at the ruins at Petra, where he negotiates the traps set to foil unworthy seekers and steps out on a ledge where he can see his goal, a cave containing the Grail. But there is a chasm too wide to cross; this gap separates him from final victory. In the movie, he steps into the void and a bridge magically appears, allowing him to walk across the gap to his goal. Of course, the gaps we face in real life have to be dealt with differently, but the treasures waiting for us when we close these gaps are very real. One of those treasures is the ability to attain inner peace.

> Inner peace comes from having serenity, balance, and harmony in our lives achieved through the disciplined closing of the Three Gaps.

Gaps in our lives drain the power needed to make a positive difference in the world. As I will discuss in this book, when we close the Three Gaps we earn the right to serenity, balance, and harmony in our lives, which will in turn increase our capacity to make a real difference in the world.

CHAPTER 1

The Beliefs Gap

Closing the Beliefs Gap

The Power of the Belief Window

Because beliefs are such a powerful determining factor in our lives, the first gap I want to discuss is the gap between what you believe to be true and what is actually true: your Beliefs Gap.

There was a time when the vast majority of the people on this earth believed that the sun revolved around the earth. When Copernicus suggested and Galileo insisted that it was the other way around, people considered them heretics. The fact that they were right was irrelevant; and, at the time, believing the wrong thing about the sun's relationship to the earth had no serious consequences (other than personal ostracism). Had we not corrected that erroneous belief we certainly would never have had the power to achieve the tremendous scientific advances spurred on by the space program. The correct belief allowed us to make a difference.

Consider the following story.

John walks into the yard of a friend, and is surprised to see a Doberman pinscher that has never been there before. At first he freezes in terror; then he runs out of the yard as fast as his legs can carry him without pausing to wonder how the dog got there or to notice if it is on a chain.

Later, Susan walks into the same yard. She is just as surprised as John to be greeted by a Doberman. Her reaction, however, is to squeal with delight, "Oh! How cute!" She runs toward the dog so she can pet it and scratch it behind its ears.

Why such different reactions to the same dog? It's all about what I call the Belief Window.

Everyone has a Belief Window. I like to picture it as a small, clear window hanging in front of your face. I imagine it hooked in place so that every time you move, the Belief Window moves with you: you look out into the world through that window and you draw in information from the world through the same window.

On this Belief Window you have placed thousands of beliefs or principles that you assume to be correct. They have accumulated over your entire life and they are not all equal in value. Some are good, some aren't. Some are rational, some are irrational. Some are productive and some are counterproductive. The number of beliefs on your Belief Window tends to be a function of your age and experience. We put beliefs on our windows because we believe that they are true and that by following them we will meet our needs over time.

John has a belief on his Belief Window that says that all Doberman pinschers are vicious; he has accepted that as a correct principle. So when he is confronted by a Doberman pinscher, his behavior is to run, to evade, to leap tall buildings with a single bound—whatever it takes to distance himself from that Doberman. He doesn't go through an analysis of the situation. Reactions based on one's underlying beliefs are automatic.

Susan, on the other hand, has a belief that says that all dogs are cute and sweet. Her behavior around a Doberman is drastically different from John's because of what she believes to be true about dogs.

Your Belief Window is covered with beliefs, and that window governs your behavior. The issue is,

> **Do you have correct or incorrect beliefs on your Belief Window?**

Everyone has correct, incorrect, and debatable beliefs that influence behavior. Keep in mind that in using the terms *correct* and *incorrect*, I am not attempting to make moral judgments about whether beliefs are "good" or "bad"; I use the terms only to simplify this discussion, and to indicate how those beliefs affect our lives.

If a belief reflects natural law or reality—such as "vegetables are good for people," "gravity keeps me on the ground," or "the world revolves around the sun"—it may be considered as generally correct. Beliefs contrary to such natural laws could be considered incorrect.

In addition to being based on natural laws, the things we believe can be reflections of personal values, such as "financial independence is important" or "I should treat others the way I want to be treated."

Beliefs can also simply be a subjective judgment or matter of opinion, such as "European cars are better than American cars," "broccoli doesn't taste good," or "I can eat anything I want and it won't affect me adversely." Matters of opinion are not easily categorized as correct or incorrect. Whether your beliefs are backed by strong scientific evidence, grow out of your values, or are completely subjective doesn't change the fact that *because we believe them to be true, we will act as if they are true.* The key is to identify the beliefs on our window and change those that are incorrect, inadequate, or counterproductive.

Because there is no way to print out a list of the beliefs on anyone's Belief Window, we need to find another way to determine what those beliefs might be. The only way to do this is to examine the behavior they produce. (It wouldn't be too hard to figure out what John has on his Belief Window about Dobermans based on observing his behavior pattern whenever he runs into one.) If you analyze a pattern of behavior in your own life that has negative results, you are the victim of an incorrect or inadequate belief. In other words, you have a Belief Gap that needs closing.

In another book, *You Are What You Believe,* I discuss more fully a model of human behavior known as the Reality Model. I will not discuss it in detail here, but will suggest that you pick up that book for a complete explanation.

It suffices here to point out that incorrect beliefs on your Belief Window lead to patterns of behavior that produce negative results. You will experience stress, emotional pain, relationship disruptions, and/or employment disappointments (among other things) when this is the case.

Let me point out here that all of our beliefs and behaviors are designed to meet basic needs common to all of us. Those generally accepted needs include the need to live (survival), the need to love and be loved (relationship), the need to feel important (have value), and the need for variety. If we are not meeting those needs, we will feel pain in one way or another. (John was no doubt trying to meet his need to live when he ran from the Doberman, and Susan was meeting her need to love and be loved.)

What is important to understand is that even though we put beliefs on our Belief Window that we think will meet these needs, we are not always correct. Perhaps because of a bad experience early in life, or because someone taught us something at an early age, or because we might misinterpret events around us, all of us get beliefs on our Belief Window that fail to meet our needs.

This is a good time to point out that determining whether or not your behavior meets your needs takes time to measure. Something that may seem to meet your needs in a one-time situation takes on a whole different dimension when measured over time. An obvious example might be the use and abuse of alcohol. If you believe that drinking relaxes you and makes you more socially adept, you may try that a few times; it may even work the way you intend it to. But many people have found that, over time, the results from that belief do great damage to their relationships, employment, and mental health. Remember, results take time to measure.

You can choose to believe whatever you wish; just remember that your beliefs drive your behavior. A correct belief will lead to good results—results that are positive and beneficial to you. In other words, it will meet one or more of your four basic needs over time. An incorrect belief will lead to bad results—results that are negative or damaging to you. It will not meet your needs over time. It's as simple as that.

Let's take another example. Let's say that you have a belief that was mentioned above: European cars are better than American cars. If that is your belief, then you set up your (invisible) behavior rules so that when it is time for you to buy a new car, your choice is rather simple. What kind of car will you buy? Behavior is automatic; it grows out of the principle that you have accepted as true on your Belief Window. Will the results of choosing to buy a European car meet your needs over time? Possibly.

Here is another example. Let's say that a belief that you hold is that you must never lose at games. If that is true for you, then when you start to lose a game, what will be the probable behavior? It could be to cheat, quit, or even throw a tantrum. It depends on the behavior rules that you set up as a result of this belief. Then the question must be asked: Will the results of this behavior meet your needs over time? Probably not, in this case. You may have to replace this belief with an alternative one in order to close the gap and create inner peace in your life.

Some examples of possible beliefs that may be on a Belief Window are:

- Schools should go back to basics.
- My self-worth is determined by things I own, the job I have, and the praise I receive from others.
- Mom and Dad will always love me regardless of what I do.
- My family will never understand me.
- Men are inferior.
- Women are inferior.
- I'm a pawn of outside forces and I can't do anything about it.
- I'm not an addict. I can quit any time.
- Some people are simply worth more than others.

Remember:

> Any belief that drives behavior that does not meet your basic needs *over time* is an incorrect belief.

The key to monitoring your Belief Window, to deciding what to accept as correct and what to adjust or discard as incorrect, is to follow these four steps:

Step 1: Admit. To begin the process, you will need to admit two things to yourself. First, you will need to admit that there is behavior in your life that is causing pain, stress, or chaos. It is often easier to identify the pain than it is to see the behavior that

is causing it, but most of us will get there if we are
honest with ourselves.

Second, you will have to admit that you must
change yourself in order to improve your life. We
all tend to externalize; we tend to blame others or
outside forces for our pain. We think it so often
that we truly believe it. A willingness to admit that
we are the problem is the key to progress. (And
because *we* are the only persons we can change,
putting the blame on others means that our pain
will not go away.)

Step 2: Ask Yourself Why. You now need to ask yourself why you are behaving in a way that leads to the
negative results noted in step 1. If you keep asking
why, and if you are honest with yourself, you will
ultimately find the answer. *And the answer to the
question "Why?" always comes up as a belief on your
Belief Window.*

Why do I run away from dogs? (I believe that
all dogs are dangerous.) Why do I make jokes at
inappropriate times? (I believe that being funny is
the best way to make friends.) Why do I cheat at
games? (I believe that my value as a person is based
on winning at games.) Why do I continue to hang
out with an abusive person? (I believe that I deserve
the abuse I receive.) Why am I always late to
meetings? (I think my time is more valuable than
that of others.)

This may take some time, and it will definitely
take some honest self-examination. You will

usually know when you have hit bedrock, when
you have surfaced the belief that is at the root of
your behavior.

Step 3: Adopt an Alternative Belief. This is the part
where you must get creative. You must identify a
new belief, one that is an alternative to the belief
that is causing your troublesome behavior. The
first example above (all dogs are dangerous) could
be replaced with a different belief (most dogs are
friendly). You can test various alternatives by
projecting how you would behave if you actually
believed the alternative principle. In this over-
simplified case, you would no longer run every
time you saw a dog; you would look forward to the
experience. (And even if you found the occasional
mean dog, it would still fit with your new belief
that *most* dogs are friendly.) If that is a better
result, better meeting your needs over time, then it
is likely that you have found the belief you need
to write on your Belief Window.

Now, this is easy to write about, but it is not as
easy to do. The reason you have a belief in the first
place is because you think it is true, and you are
now trying to substitute something you don't
think is true. Move on to the next step, and you
will see how this can work.

Step 4: Act as If. Up to this point, everything has
been an academic exercise. You have examined your
stress points and have tied them to behaviors that
produce them. You have asked yourself why you

behave that way, and examined the beliefs that dictate your behavior. But none of that has required you to change anything.

You are now at that point. But how do you change a belief that could be the product of years of reinforcement? Once you identify an alternative belief, even if you "know" it can't be true, you take the most important and most difficult step. You begin to act *as if* the new belief is true.

Neuroscience has taught us that behavior creates neural pathways in the brain. By acting a certain way over and over, those actions begin to feel normal. This is sometimes known as "fake it till you make it." In the beginning, it will take conscious thought to do this. Over time, it becomes easier and, ultimately, automatic.

I will promise you this: once the belief has been changed, the behavior it produces automatically changes with it. And the pain caused by the old behavior goes away.

> Remember, until you change the belief on your Belief Window, your behavior will never change.

Your Belief Window and the Belief Gap

Anytime you're getting results that are causing long-term harm, such as missing promotions, experiencing unemployment, losing important relationships, struggling with your weaknesses or addictions, or any other form of missing out on things that are important to you, your Belief

Gap—the gap between what you believe will meet your needs and what will actually do so—is too wide. As a result, you are like Indiana Jones, stranded on the wrong side of a chasm. You are not in a position to make a positive difference in the world, and it's time for a change.

The key to closing the Beliefs Gap is being able to put into practice the four steps outlined above. The results in your life flow automatically from your behavior, and that behavior is a function of the beliefs on your Belief Window. This all happens automatically, without even consciously thinking about it; but what you allow on your Belief Window is the key.

> If you want results that meet your needs over time,
> change the beliefs on your Belief Window!

You close the gap by changing the belief. When the belief changes, everything changes.

Change is almost never instantaneous. It can, at times, feel like two steps forward and one step back. But as you continue to act with your new belief, positive results will occur and you will know that you have closed a gap between something you *believed* would meet your needs and something that *actually will*.

Always ask yourself this critical question:

> Will this behavior meet my needs over time?

If the answer is anything but a sincere and confident *yes*, then begin surgery on your Belief Window.

Tyler and Jennifer Wilkinson

I've known Tyler for many years; he attended high school with my son, and was one of the best high school running backs ever to come out of the state of Utah. In my opinion, Tyler and his wife Jennifer are probably the most powerful and compelling example I have ever known of two people who were willing to close the Belief Gap.

Tyler and Jennifer have had to deal with an immense tragedy in their lives and decided that they were not going to be beat by it. They had to examine what they believed about themselves and their opportunities in the world.

What follows is their story. You will see how changing beliefs became fundamental to their lives as they evolved. As I spoke with them about the power of closing the Belief Gap, their responses were so natural and free-flowing that I decided to let them share their experience with you, the reader, just as they shared it with me.

(Tyler) I grew up with two older brothers, who were athletes, and three younger sisters. Being five and a half and three and a half years younger than my brothers, I looked up to them. And sports were important to me too; anything I could do to impress them was a big deal to me, the little brother. We lived in a small town, and I always wanted to be a football player and a baseball player.

I always felt that I was competing against not just the people locally but with other kids all over America who were getting up early, doing pushups and sit-ups, and running. I always kind of looked over my shoulder. With that focus, I improved and became a better athlete. My dad and mom supported me in sports. Of course, they also wanted me to do well academically. I did okay; I recognized that it was important. I got 3.3s, 3.4s, and occasionally 3.5 or 3.6 maybe even a 3.7 grade point average, but if it came down to a homework assignment versus athletic practice, I chose the practice. My parents recognized that my hard work could pay off in a scholarship.

As I got into middle school, I started getting interested in social life quite a bit more. I met Jennifer in eighth grade and kind of started liking her in ninth grade. Now, I think I recognized in Jennifer attributes that I felt were different from those of other girls. There were a lot of neat girls around, but Jennifer just carried herself differently; she seemed to live the standards that I hoped for. Even though we were young, we associated with each other a lot. We did date other people, but we were often together with just each other. I did feel like there was a maturity in our relationship. Even during high school, we talked about what things we felt mattered most. I obviously understood that faith was very important to her, and those values and things associated with our faith were important to me as well.

(Jennifer) I am the oldest of five kids, and we grew up in small-town America. I had a very similar childhood to Tyler's. We did start dating—well, we started "liking each other"—in ninth grade. So we actually dated for six years before we got married. I feel we had a level of maturity in our relationship that maybe a lot of high school couples don't have.

We weren't that lovey-dovey high school couple. I mean, we liked each other for about three years before the accident, but we hadn't ever said, "I love you" to each other. We just felt like that was a little premature—like that was a serious kind of adult thing, to really fall in love with somebody.

We just tried to keep our relationship a little more on a friend level in some ways. So my thoughts were always that I would graduate from high school and go to college. I was never a great student. I got similar grades as Tyler, and education wasn't my highest priority. My mom loved being a mom—at least I felt like she did. She told me many times that she loved being a stay-at-home mom, and that's what I wanted to do. I didn't have career goals or aspirations; I thought that if I needed to work, I could be a teacher or work with kids somehow.

In high school I was excited about someday getting married, picking the colors for my reception. I kind of pictured my future husband. I don't know if you know this, but girls sometimes live in a fantasy land. I remember dreaming about my husband carrying me across the threshold on our wedding night.

(Tyler) Just a couple of weeks before my accident, in the middle of our senior year, I met with the football and baseball coaches at our local university. I signed a letter with them to play both baseball and football. Other schools had shown interest in me, and I had gone on some recruiting trips, but this school would pay for everything; plus, I was going to be able to play both sports. Everything was lining up.

That Saturday morning I got into my dad's truck. Jennifer was dancing for the high school drill team, and I planned to hang out with her family that day. I was excited about our relationship, about my prospects for the upcoming baseball season; everything was good. Then I fell asleep at the wheel. The truck rolled, and my life changed dramatically.

(Jennifer) We were at the state championship for our drill team. February 16, 1991. I didn't know if Tyler was coming; he still wasn't sure when we left. And, because it was before cell phones, we had no way of knowing. I was in the middle of our competition; we had done a couple of our dances when my mom found out Tyler had been in an accident. She didn't immediately come and tell me because she knew my team needed me to stay focused, and she knew there was nothing that we could do right then to help him.

(Tyler) I was lying there in my truck, suspended in the air by my seatbelt, with my arms out in front of me. My arms were jerking up and down; I didn't have any control over them. In my mind, I was temporarily paralyzed and in shock, but then things really started to kind of hit me: this could be a lot more serious than just being in shock and temporarily paralyzed.

When I was a kid growing up, I had a neighbor two houses down who had broken her back. She was maybe in her early twenties. My friends and I would play football and baseball on their lawn, and I remember seeing her transferring out of the wheelchair and into the car. Years later, as I hung upside down in my own car, I remember that I thought I would rather be dead than in a wheelchair; I wouldn't be able to play ball any more.

Fear just started to cave in on me. There I was, waiting for the ambulance, thinking that this might be a spinal cord injury. Then I remember waiting for the Life Flight helicopter to take me to the closest major trauma hospital. I asked the local doctor to pray for me. I don't remember what he said, but I remember I thought everything would be okay. I didn't think that twenty-something years later "okay" would include me still in a wheelchair.

It is interesting how our beliefs change. We have to evolve in how we see ourselves. When the helicopter landed, I knew I would never play football or baseball again.

Still, I thought I was going to work so hard. I was going to have this drive. It didn't matter what the doctor said, I was just going to work and work my way out of it. But every day that passed, it got harder and harder to say that things were going to get better.

I remember thinking about a poem that Hyrum used to quote, by Henry Van Dyke, about a sundial:

The shadow by my finger cast
Divides the future from the past:
. . . .
Behind its unreturning line,
The vanished hour no longer thine . . .

That's kind of how I started thinking. I started thinking okay, maybe I can't walk out of here tomorrow or the next day, but maybe I can get off this ventilator.

(Jennifer) As soon as my mom came and told me, I started to cry. I remember being alarmed by my reaction. I wasn't superdramatic in high school; I wasn't a girlie-girl in that way. I didn't react to things like that; I was more low key and mellow. Those tears began to show me how strong my feelings were for Tyler.

My mom and I took off at that point; we drove up to Salt Lake, to the hospital where Tyler was. We spent the next few days there just trying to make sure he was okay. I think we stayed through the weekend and then came home.

It was a little bit difficult coming home and going back to school, because everybody loved Tyler. He was such a great athlete, and a really nice person. He was popular not only for the things he did but also because of how he treated people.

The following Monday, on my way to school, I had to drive past the baseball field. I knew how much Tyler loved baseball, and the season was just starting. I started to cry. I knew things would never be the same. I mean, spring was an exciting time; baseball season was just starting, and there is just something about that. And yet I just felt so sad for him. I didn't feel sorry for him; I just felt sad that he had to go through this really difficult time and his life was changing so drastically. He couldn't do those things that he loved anymore.

During all this time, our relationship just continued to move forward; we had to figure some things out. I remember something when he was in the intensive care unit. I don't know if I was helping him eat, or maybe he was in rehab. I said something about helping feed my kids, like I was practicing to help feed my kids. I wasn't saying it in a rude way, because to me it was kind of like a temporary thing; I didn't think this would be something I always had to do.

He did not like that very much, so we had little bumps in the road like that, but for the most part I believe that we both worked through everything together, took things as they were; and with time it all worked out.

(Tyler) I left town, and I was, like, mister athlete. When I came home, I was meeting all of my peers again, all of my classmates, and I didn't know if I wanted to eat in front of my peers because I had a special fork that's strapped onto my hand, and I still wasn't very good at hitting my mouth every time.

So I went from being like any other high school kid, and then—*boom!*—I had a fork strapped to my hand to eat. My life had been so defined by accomplishing things on a football field or baseball field; I remember wondering, how do I redefine who I am and the relationship I have with so many people?

A family friend who owned an airplane volunteered to fly me home from the hospital. I will never forget the moment we landed; a group of friends had come out to greet me. After talking for a bit, my dad put me in his car; we turned left, while all of my friends who had piled in a different vehicle turned right on their way to the lake. I felt like that's where I should be; I should be with them, going that direction, but instead I was going to rehab. I remember that being kind of a real wake-up call, a dose of reality: this is your life. Life wasn't fun for a couple of years after the accident. Then things finally started to change.

After the accident, I still wanted to graduate from college, and I wanted to get married to a wonderful person and have a family and a career. These were all the goals I had before my accident, and they were still my goals after it. I realized it was good to have those goals, but in the short term all I could really do was focus on what I was going to do each day. I got off the ventilator, and I got to where I could start sitting up in the chair, where I could start to feed myself with the assisted technology. Then I eventually started to push my chair, and things were progressing, though much slower than what I had hoped for. Then I began to believe I could rebuild my life and work on those original dreams.

My family was a great support; my friends were a great support, but Jennifer—she came up every single weekend, and as much as I loved my family and my friends, I worked all week long so that when Jennifer came she could see my efforts, because she made such a big deal out of just little incremental improvements.

(Jennifer) I wasn't like a cheerleader. If you watch the movie about him, it portrays me as going, "Oh! You can do it." I'm just not that way. I was just supportive, and I would say, "Good job."

(Tyler) She noticed things. Even when she said she was sad that she couldn't watch me play, she was much more sad for me. She was sad even more for my father, who she knew would never see me play again. She just made me feel great. And in the little progress that I would make, I knew was going to be rewarded by her, just by her subtle comments and how just great she was.

(Jennifer) And he was hoping for lots of kisses and stuff.

(Tyler) Well, I thought there would be some affection; that was a major motivator. In the many times

I figuratively and literally fell on my face, I found the strength to get back up; it was due to her.

You have got to just get back up and keep going. Some of these beliefs, obviously, were instilled in me from my family—from my parents and my brothers. And from working hard in athletics—that things are hard, things were hard in athletics; that life is a challenge, and you are going to fall on your face. You are going to get tackled, or you are going to get hurt, and you just have to get up and keep going. That was the philosophy that kept me trying. But I have to say that Jen was a huge motivator.

(Jennifer) Before we got married, we had discussed everything that was going to have to happen in order for me to help him, to take care of him. His parents had been taking care of him, helping him with all of the things that he couldn't do by himself: getting up in the morning, getting dressed, getting showered, all that kind of stuff.

I knew what I was going to be helping him with; then we got married. When we actually started living together and I was his primary caregiver, it was a lot harder than I thought it was going to be.

I believed I needed to just suck it up and get things done—just do my duty, I guess. I was going to school, dancing on the college dance team, working full-time, and helping him. It was kind of going okay, but I kept thinking, I can't do all of this.

I felt like I put myself in a position where I was basically on call for him twenty-four hours a day. It wasn't even his fault; it was my own, but being so wrapped up in caring for him I kind of lost myself, which put me in a place that was really difficult for me.

Finally I had to step up and say, "Something has got to change here." So I got a new job, and we ended up having some help come in. They would help him get up just a few days a week, just so that we could have a relationship. We were off balance. We were so off balance at that point that—and I had let myself get to that point—I was really discouraged and a bit depressed. We had to just make changes to make it better. It actually worked.

(Tyler) One night we kind of got into an argument, and all of a sudden for the first time in six months, she got way emotional. She just said, "I don't know if I can do this anymore." I thought that for the first time we were actually communicating.

She had kind of bottled it up and then let me have it all one night. I mean, looking back, it was obvious, but at the time I was kind of clueless. I was oblivious, because I am kind of clueless. She helped me realize how things really were, as opposed to how

I saw them through my Belief Window. I learned so many great lessons from her, and now we do a lot better. We don't let things go on for extended periods of time; that's something that we've tried to keep in check throughout our whole marriage.

(Jennifer) Yes, we keep things in check; we keep a balance. Periodically we will get into a rut where he starts asking us to help him with things that he can do himself. We have to take a step back and say, "Okay. It's time for you to start doing this again." Luckily, we have come to a point where I don't have to get mad and he doesn't have to get offended when that happens because we both want to make each other happy. If one of us is not happy with the situation, we both are willing to make changes in what we believe, what we expect, and what we do for ourselves and for each other.

We are equal partners, but I have noticed one thing in our relationship. As we have gone through our marriage, learning different things, we just have had different experiences.

I never dreamed of arriving at my wedding in a wheelchair accessible van. I drove, and he sat in his wheelchair beside me. That just wasn't the dream; that's just not a dream a teenage girl has. I never got carried across the threshold, but I built a life—*our* life—with the person of my dreams, and with all the ups and downs it has been such a beautiful life.

(Tyler) I don't think that our life is really that much different from anybody else's life. I don't wake up and go, "I am still paralyzed." I don't wake up and just think, "What are all the bad things happening in my life?" We just get up each day and this is how life is; we just do it. But there are times we feel more *paralyzed*; I use that term because there are times when things just feel harder, when we have trouble moving forward just like everyone else does at different times in their lives.

One of my challenges, one of our family's challenges, is out there for the whole world to see. I am paralyzed. We have dozens of stories like this one.

One day was with my oldest son, who was at the time four years old. He was sitting on my lap, and I was reading a book to him. I turned pages of a book by licking my right pinky knuckle; it sticks to the page, then I turn the page. So this time with my four-year-old, I licked my finger; it stuck; and I went to turn the page, and it slipped. I did it the second time, and it slipped. When I licked my finger again, a third time, it slipped. At that point my four-year-old looked up at me from my lap, and he said, "You can't do anything." I am sure I did not handle this the right way, but I looked at him, and I said, "I can read. Can you read?"

And he looked at me again; he kind of got that sheepish look on his face and was, like, "No." And I said, "Okay, so how about you turn the pages, and I will read the story?" And he thought it sounded like a great idea, and then we finished the book.

But there are so many little things like that in everybody's life where it's a little decision point. I would love to go out in the backyard and play catch; I would love to go fly a kite. Oh my gosh! My son was trying to fly a kite, and down the street other dads were flying kites with their sons. My son couldn't get the tail hooked on, so his kite would go up, and it would crash; it would go up, and it would crash. He was so frustrated. He turned around; I was sitting on the porch watching, and he looked at me and said, "Man, all I got is a guy in a wheelchair."

When I tell this story to people, they respond, "Oh, man!" as if my kid had just shoved me under the bus, as if that's the rudest thing any person can ever say. At the time I just said, "Come over here." He came over and somehow, in some way, I was able to clip the tail on, and he looked at me, like, "Okay, you are good for something." We live in a world where people take offense at everything. If I was ultrasensitive about being disabled, or this or that, I guess I could just curl up in the fetal position and life would kind of pass me by. But we have chosen a different road, and it has made all the difference.

Tyler and Jennifer have five children. Tyler is a highly respected financial management executive, and Jennifer is the mom she always dreamed of being. Together they are doing what matters most to them.

Remember Indiana Jones? For the Belief Gap, the cave with the Holy Grail represents correct principles. The ledge at the edge of the chasm represents what you believe to be true. When you cross that chasm so that what you believe to be true merges into what *is* actually true, you have earned the right to inner peace.

CHAPTER 2

The Values Gap

Closing the Values Gap

It's not uncommon in this crazy hectic world to get so caught up in the "busy-ness" of life that, before you know it, time has passed; and when you look back you might feel as if a piece of your life has gone missing.

You usually come to this kind of realization when something major happens, such as watching a child leave home, having a heart attack, going through a divorce, having problems with a struggling business, watching the economy go off a cliff, dealing with a rebellious child, or witnessing something that you've always believed, trusted, or known fail in some way. Time feels as if it comes to a standstill, and you pause for self-reflection.

When you find yourself in one of these situations you can become painfully aware of a gap between what you value most and what you are actually doing—the Values Gap. Where are you actually spending your time, energy, and resources compared to where you *want* to be spending them? The Values Gap is the gap between doing "any old thing" and doing the things that matter most.

You might look back and wonder how things could possibly get so far off the rails without you having noticed, or whether you could have made a more significant difference. What if there was a way to get caught off guard by life less often? What if there was a way to prepare proactively rather than regret retroactively? What if you could decide for yourself rather than having life decide for you?

The key to getting to a place of purposeful living lies in understanding the Values Gap. Understand this fact: everyone has a set of what I call *governing values*. These values answer the question of which priorities should be the highest for you, and they ultimately govern every aspect of your life.

> Governing values are simply a description
> of one's highest priorities.

Your governing values should be important enough to you that you will invest your time, resources, and energy in making them a fundamental part of your life.

Remember, whenever there is a gap between what you value and what you are doing, you are in pain. For example, if you value being physically fit, and you weigh three hundred pounds, there is a gap between what you value and what you are actually doing, and you are in pain. If you value being financially stable, and you are half a million dollars in debt, you are in pain.

If you want inner peace on either of these values, you have to close the Values Gap.

The "busy-ness" of life distracts us from the realization of these values and gets us off the track we want to be on—usually without us being fully aware that it's happening. We invest time, resources, and energy in things that are not really of value to us. Then when something major happens, we step back a moment and realize the mistakes we've made. We can then feel deeply betrayed.

Closing the Values Gap—between what you value most and what you are actually doing—will enable you to make a powerful difference in the world around you.

There are three simple but necessary steps that must be followed to close the Values Gap:

Step 1: Identify Your Governing Values. To start, let me share a simple exercise that I have used for nearly four decades to help people discover their true governing values; I call it the I-Beam Experience. It's merely a starting point; its purpose is not to answer the entire question of what your values are, but it will help you begin the journey of discovery.

I've shared this concept with hundreds of audiences all around the world, and I'll tell you before we start that the reaction is universally the same. When I am teaching this in a public seminar, I always ask someone in the audience who has a child under the age of two to help me, and with this person I walk through the following scenario. Put yourself in the place of this audience member; for our purposes, we will call him George.

"George, what is the name of your two-year-old?" I ask.

"Madison," George responds.

"Okay, I'm going to ask you a few questions, and by your answers, we are going to discover one of your governing values.

"I have lying out here in front of the building an I-beam that is three hundred feet long. This is an unusually long I-beam. In case you don't know what an I-beam is, it's a piece of structural steel used in framing large buildings such as skyscrapers. If you look at it from one end you will see that it looks like a capital letter *I*. If you turn it on its side, it becomes an H-beam. I'm going to put you at one end of the I-beam, and I'll be at the other end."

I now take a hundred-dollar bill out of my pocket, and I say, "George, if you'll come across this I-beam without stepping off either side and get here in two minutes, I'll give you a hundred dollars. Would you come?"

George hesitates a minute.

"It's on the ground, George," I remind him.

"Oh yeah, of course I would come."

"All right, now we're going to change the scenario a little bit. We're going to put the I-beam on the back of a long, flatbed truck and drive it over to the North Rim of the Grand Canyon. There is a place there three hundred feet across, and it is

1,160 feet straight down. We're going to bolt the I-beam in to each wall of the canyon. It is perfectly safe, it will hold tons of weight. It is, however, a little bowed because of the expanse. And it's raining—not very hard, just sort of a thick mist. There is also a wind blowing at about forty miles per hour.

"George, you are on one side of the chasm, and I am on the other. I shout through the wind and the rain, 'If you'll come across this I-beam without stepping off either side, and get here in two minutes, I'll give you a hundred dollars. Would you come now?'"

"No!"

"Okay, I now have ten thousand dollars. Unmarked bills. The money is yours the minute you get to my end. Would you come for ten thousand dollars?"

"No."

"How about fifty thousand dollars? There won't be any taxes taken out of it. All you have to do is walk the same three hundred feet you walked back there on the sidewalk. Would you risk that for fifty thousand dollars?"

There is a pause before George says, "No, I don't think I would."

"All right, let's change the scenario again. I have one million dollars. The rain has picked up, and the wind is blowing at about sixty miles per hour, but this is a million dollars. Would you risk it for a million dollars?"

Now George is thinking about it. "Are there any safety devices?" he asks.

"No."

"How wide is the I-beam again?"

"Six inches."

"It's windy and rainy?"

"Yes."

"No, I don't think I'd do it," George says.

I say, "Okay, we'll change the scenario one more time. I'm not a nice guy anymore, George. I'm holding your two-year-old, Madison, by the hair and dangling her over the edge of the canyon. If you don't get across that I-beam right now, I'm going to drop Madison. Would you come now?"

He immediately responds, "Yes, I would."

There is a lot of emotion now. We just discovered one of George's governing values: "I love my child." Safety has value, money has value, but of a much higher value is the love of the child. George would probably risk the I-beam, the danger of the chasm, the wind and the rain, for his daughter. And this is what governing values are really all about.

I once performed the I-Beam Experience with a woman who had a teenager. She wouldn't come across for the teenager.

When you sit down to identify your governing values, the highest, deepest, most valued priorities in your life, you must ask yourself this question:

What would I cross the I-beam for?

What value, idea, principle, or person has such great value to you that you would risk, maybe even dedicate your life to that value? Dedication is a whole lot tougher than risking, because it takes time.

Twenty years ago, I ran through the I-Beam Experience with a group in Hong Kong. I picked a man out of the audience who had a child under the age of two. This man turned out to be from India. I set the situation up, describing the I-beam on the ground, and asked, "Would you come across for a hundred dollars?"

"No, I wouldn't," he said.

"Wait a minute," I said. "It's on the ground, why wouldn't you come for a hundred dollars?"

"I don't do that kind of stuff for money," he said.

"Well, I've got the wrong guy."

The man sitting next to him had a two-year-old daughter, so I asked him if he would come across the I-beam on the ground for a hundred dollars. He said he would, and so I walked him through the rest of the scenario.

When I got to the part about coming across the I-beam or losing his two-year-old, the man from India was on the edge of his seat. After the other man acknowledged that he would definitely come across for his child, I looked over at the man from India.

I asked, "How about you? Would you come across the I-beam now?"

"Damn right I would," he said. "And I would kill you when I got to the other side."

The audience laughed.

The I-Beam Experience will get you emotionally involved in the discovery process. You must now ask yourself a question: What would I cross the I-beam for? What is that important to me? That is where you start.

Step 2: Write a Clarifying Statement Describing Exactly What Your Governing Values Mean to You. After you have identified and written down your governing values—your highest priorities—write a clarifying statement for each value, describing exactly what it means to you.

An example of what this might look like was sent to me by a seminar participant. One of her governing values was health, and she wrote this clarifying statement:

Health

I work out three times a week.
I limit fast food to no more than once a week.
I improve the quality of time spent on weekends.
I laugh or smile more often.
I identify and mitigate stress sources.

Another participant wrote her clarifying statement in an entirely different way:

I Grow Intellectually

I listen with an open mind to what people have to say and take in from their comments what I think will enhance my world. I read things related to all aspects of my life (job, kids, the world in general) and seek to internalize worthwhile things. I seek opportunities for formal education that will help me learn and grow. I learn everything I can about my department and company that will enhance my ability to do a better job.

As you can see, there is no "right" way to write a clarifying statement, as long as it states in some way what each governing value means to you.

Step 3: Prioritize Your Governing Values. Now rank your governing values in order of their importance to you. I can't stress enough the importance of taking the time to prioritize this list; it is the most important list you will ever work with. The reason will become clear through the following story.

Herman Krannert was living in Indianapolis in 1925. He was an executive for the Sefton Container Company. On one occasion, he was summoned to Chicago to have lunch with the president of the company; he was very excited because he had never been invited to do so before.

During lunch the president said, "Herman, I'm going to make an announcement in the company this afternoon that greatly impacts your life. We're going to promote you to senior executive vice president, and you're to be the newest member of the board of directors."

Krannert was blown away. He said, "Sir, I had no idea I was even being considered for this. I want you to know I'll be the most loyal employee this company has ever had. I'm going to dedicate my life to making this the finest corporation in America."

The president was gratified by this and said, "You know, Herman, I'm glad you mentioned that because there's one thing I'd like you to remember. As a member of the board of directors you will vote exactly the way I tell you to."

That took some wind out of Krannert's sails, and he said he wasn't sure he could do that.

"Come on, Herman, that's the way it is in the business world. I'm putting you on the board of directors. You'll do what I tell you, right?"

The more Krannert thought about that, the angrier he became. At the end of lunch he stood up and said, "I need you to understand I cannot accept this promotion. I will not be a puppet on the board of directors for anybody." Then he added, "Not only that, I don't think I want to work for a company where such demands are made. I quit."

He returned to Indianapolis that night, approached his wife, and said, "You'll be excited to know that today I was promoted to senior executive vice president, made a member of the board of directors, and I quit."

She said, "You *quit*? Have you lost your mind?"
Upon hearing the explanation, she understood and
supported his decision. "Well, I guess we'll have to
find something else."

Four nights later a knock came at his door. Six
senior executives from his company burst through
the door, all excited. "Herman, we heard what
happened the other day. We think that's the greatest
thing we've ever heard. In fact, we quit too."

"What do you mean, you quit too?" he asked.

"Yeah, we quit too, and here's the good news.
We're going to go to work for *you!*"

"How are you going to work for me? I don't even
have a job."

"Oh, we figure you'll find something, and when
you do, we're going to work for you."

That night those seven people sat down at
Herman Krannert's dining room table and created
the Inland Container Corporation. It became a
multibillion-dollar empire because, in 1925, a guy
not only knew what his governing values were, but
prioritized them. One of them was loyalty; another
was integrity, but he had prioritized integrity above
loyalty. How different would his life have been had
he prioritized them in the other order?

Your Personal Constitution

Now you can see why prioritizing your governing values
list is one of the most important steps you can take in
closing the Values Gap. What do you suppose the U.S.

Constitution is to the people of the United States? It represents our set of values as a people—complete with clarifying statements. No law in the United States is ever ratified until it is measured against the Constitution and deemed to be consistent with the founding fathers' intentions.

After you go through these three steps—identify, clarify, prioritize—what will you have done? You will have written your own personal constitution. What kinds of things might you include in your list of governing values?

First, let's be clear on one thing: I would never presume to tell you what your values ought to be; that's none of my business. I can, however, tell you that you have values already in place. Having taught this lesson for the last forty years, I have discovered that there are probably five or six values that are regularly expressed as high priorities by the thousands of people I've worked with.

Some of these values include:

- family and relationships
- physical wellness
- financial wellness
- education
- integrity
- making a difference

Just about everyone would agree that at least some of these are part of his or her governing values. If one of these values is also one of yours, start there and begin the process.

Completing the Process

With your values identified, clarified, and prioritized, consider the gap between what you value most and what you actually do in life. In what ways are you living your values? In what ways are you missing the mark? Starting today, what changes could you make that would start closing some gaps in specific areas of your life?

The I-Beam Experience is intended to start the process of identifying what is truly most important to you; quite frankly, it can seem a bit heavy. When I am totally honest with myself, I realize that, although they are important to me, not all of my values are so important that I would risk my life for them. But I would for some of them—especially any that deal with my family.

In the appendix you will find my personal constitution comprising sixteen governing values. This is included only as an example; your personal constitution will probably look very different from mine.

Notice that I state my values and their explanations as affirmations. I am not perfect, and I certainly don't live up to all of my stated values—*yet*. But I find it helpful to imagine myself as I want to be, so I write my value statements as if I have already achieved harmony between what I value and what I actually do.

The state of harmony between what you value and what you do will lead to inner peace. This can only be achieved when you reach down deep into your core and discover what matters most. If you don't do that, you will be living in the reactive and not the proactive world. And people who live in the reactive world lead out-of-control lives.

If you really want to close the Values Gap, ask yourself,

> What would I cross the I-beam for?
> What matters most to me?

Take the time to identify, clarify, and prioritize your values. Make a firm commitment to write your own personal constitution.

And if you want to go a step further, get your spouse or significant other to write one, and write a personal constitution with your entire family. Then step back and discover the inner peace that you will all experience together.

Linda Clemons

I met Linda Clemons at a professional women's conference in Dallas in the summer of 2013. We became dear friends after just a few conversations, and since then we have worked together as professional speakers on a number of occasions.

Linda, an African American, refers to me as "her brother from a different mother." I agree; we have a great deal in common, including many shared beliefs, a deep and abiding desire to make a difference in the world, and powerful experiences in closing the Values Gap.

On June 4, 1996, Linda finished her shift as a morning show personality on WTLC radio in Indianapolis. Later that morning she had a simple surgical procedure. Because of a problem during the surgery, she did not regain consciousness for more than a month. When she woke from the coma, Linda looked at her world through a fundamentally changed Belief Window. She began to have regular and thoughtful conversations around certain questions: What am I doing with my life? What should I be doing with my life? What are my priorities? Am I living my life in line with those priorities?

When thinking about her values before the coma, Linda cannot recall if she felt she had a gap in her life then; she had not given it a lot of thought. But coming face-to-face with her mortality lead her to thoughtfully and prayerfully consider her priorities.

Linda has shared with me the outcome of that exploration—how she wants to live her life in the future—and says, "The values that became important to me as I really pondered my life's priorities going forward were faith, family, compassion, honor, integrity, love, benevolence, commitment, and the courage to stay the course."

Although the real probing experience with her values began when she awoke from her coma, those values were actually molding who Linda was and what she would do with her life at a much earlier age.

Here, in her own words, are Linda's comments about what she has learned.

(Linda) I am the oldest of four children. Growing up, the biggest influences on my life—who I was and who I was becoming—were my mother and grandmother.

These were strong, hardworking women. They worked for what they had, and, although it wasn't always a lot, they had formed the framework to teach us what matters most in life.

Like I said, we didn't have a lot. That meant we had to make difficult choices. I remember one year, when we were young, my mother explained that my younger brother needed a new coat. I had entered a contest at school selling candy; the grand prize was a new bike, but the winner could choose a cash option. Because my brother needed a coat so badly at that time, my mother asked me to take the cash prize so she could use the money for the coat. You can imagine my disappointment. I remember my mother using that and other difficult moments to teach me an important value—one that infuses my life and my soul to this very day.

She taught me that too many people live in the "fast food lane" of life, that the desire to have everything they want right now is ruining their lives and their futures. My mother and grandmother taught me the power of being grateful for and happy with "just enough." To this day, whenever I start thinking about not having something, not receiving something, or not being recognized or valued as much as I would like, I hear their voices reaching across the years, reminding me that I am blessed, truly blessed, with "just enough" for what I really need.

I have learned to value the givers more than the gift and to recognize in their sacrifice—whether that giver was my mother, grandmother, the Lord, or anyone else—that the greater gift is the fact that they had given rather than *what* they had given.

As my mother and grandmother steered me away from the "fast food lane" of immediate gratification and reminded me to focus on having "just enough" and rejoicing in the giver regardless of the gift, I learned the power of and value in delayed gratification—such as waiting for a new bike so my brother could be warm.

As a professional adult with a responsibility to coach and lift others, the lessons from my childhood and the values they conveyed have been so critical so many times. They have helped me to teach others to value waiting, to celebrate the blessings in their lives, and to recognize that "just enough" is often far more than many, many other people ever have.

It started with a coat—a trigger to learning the values of "just enough," focusing on the giver, delaying gratification while knowing that, when the time and situation were right, the things I really needed would come to me. These were some of my earliest experiences with building a set of personal values that would accompany me on this journey through life. They've been important in many moments, at many junctures; my telling of my story and living my values has also helped others to learn these same great lessons—lessons taught to me by a strong mother and grandmother who showed through substantial personal sacrifice that they knew what to value. They blessed me with those insights.

Chia Pets

Most things, especially in the media, change often across the arc of our lifetime. One that never seems to change—in fact won't go away—are the seasonal advertisements (usually at Christmastime) for Chia Pets, those clay heads of cartoon characters, small animals, or even political figures. Each kit contains the clay figure, which needs to be soaked overnight in water, followed by a paste of soil and seeds to smear all over the figure. If the Chia Pet is kept properly watered—not too much or too little—the seeds sprout and create a pretty, green fringe that brings the hard edged, clay figure into a soft, natural beauty. That's the Chia Pet: from dead clay to living green— in a few weeks—with the right attention.

I think that those little seeds, waiting to be born, represent our values. In each seed, as in each value, is the potential for life, but only if it is properly nurtured. If our values remain as ideas in our mind or words on a page they are just seeds—ideas with the potential to close the gaps in our lives. But if we want them to go to work and help us close gaps, we must nourish them, feed them, and help them come to life.

There are a lot of ways to nurture our values, to bring them to life. We can, of course, do that nurturing on our own, through our own thoughts and efforts. But in my experience, our values flourish earlier, grow faster, and become a lasting, living part of our lives much more powerfully, when others are involved in tending to the growth of those values.

Family is one key to nurturing values. My mother and grandmother taught me the framework of my earliest values: strength, resilience, faith, and hard work. They shared with me both the experiences and the lessons that conveyed those values; they helped the values sink deep into my soul. Family feeds our bodies and then feeds our souls. Family helps us get beyond just surviving and helps us learn how to thrive—how to go from being worried about the gap between dinnertime and enough dinner to eat or the gap that comes with delaying gratification.

But what happens with people who have no family, or those who are in a dysfunctional family—one that can't get beyond survival, that might even be cruel or abusive? Who's going to water and feed that child's values and aspirations? I've spent my life around people who had less-than-complete or less-than-ideal families. And I've seen extended family members rise up in all kinds of places to fill gaps—grandmothers helping mothers where fathers have deserted them, fathers without wives present, and children without parents being raised by grandparents. I've seen extended family—aunts, uncles, cousins, neighbors, pastors and priests, and community leaders—step in to fill the gaps in both formal and informal ways. And I've watched them nurture children—not just filling their basic survival needs, but answering the deep longing to be something, to achieve their dreams, to find what they value and to live it.

Families are God's nurturers. Reach out; be part of someone's life. Help others find their way, their own values, and guide them through life's ups and downs. If you've been blessed with a family to help guide you and you can become a family for someone not so blessed, it will bless your life as well.

When you become family to someone, you release your own values into their world and the world at large. When you practice kindness, when you release it, it spreads; it grows, and it changes lives. This is one of the greatest paths to inner peace—to release your values through personal service to others. Because when people are being nurtured, their need to be recognized, accepted, acknowledged—even loved—is met. And when they hear "You're smart, you're a nice person, you're

hardworking" they flourish, and the values embedded in those statements begin to frame their
lives.

Of course, the opposite is also true. Those values
need attention and proper nurturing. Remember
that Chia Pet? If you put the seed mixture on the
dry Chia Pet and ignore it, what life there might
have been in the seeds will die as they shrivel and
dry. If people are isolated, if their values are not
nurtured, they will die too—first on the inside,
where all their goodness was waiting to get out, to
be shared, and to make a difference.

Now, it's not only others who need watering.
Some of us have ourselves gone kind of dead inside. Some of us need to find, or even rediscover,
the values we have. Some of us are damaged. Life
has been unkind, even brutal to some, and in fight-
ing against that brutality we've lost touch with or
stopped believing in ourselves.

We can get beyond the hurt and start to heal the
scars. And one of the best ways to start is by looking
at our values—what we would cross the I-beam for.

When you're at the bottom of the deepest, dark-
est, scariest hole, you'd do almost anything to get
out, to get up into the light of a better day. The
I-beam can help you out, get you beyond the dark-
ness of the moment. Think about what you'd cross
the I-beam for, and then get up on it and start

walking. In your case it might not be a beam lying on the ground or stretching horizontally across two points; it might be a ladder up and out of the hole you've fallen into. Whatever it is, you've got to get on it, get past the fear of falling off it, and use your values as the way up and out.

The Glass Ceiling

A friend of mine recently had the opportunity in her organization to break through the glass ceiling—to get an executive-level job, which, as a woman, had eluded her for some years. The selection process was proceeding smoothly. There was one other candidate, also a woman, under consideration, but my friend was confident that in the end her own qualifications would land her the position.

One day, the other candidate came to my friend and asked for some confidential, personal advice. In the process of asking for that advice, this other woman revealed some things about herself that might negatively impact her getting the job. Although the challenge this candidate revealed would not have legally or ethically prevented her promotion, it would likely have swayed the decision makers to remove her from consideration.

My friend had a choice to make. She could reveal, intentionally or accidentally, what she had learned—even in a way that would separate her from the leak.

Or she could keep it to herself and run the risk that, with the weakness unknown, the other candidate would beat her out for the job.

She said nothing, and the other woman got the promotion. A few weeks later, I was talking with my friend about her losing the promotion and I learned the whole story—as I've just shared it with you. We talked about the tremendous courage and character my friend had shown; we talked of her values of maintaining personal confidences and being trustworthy; we recognized how living those values had cost her the job.

A few months later my friend called up, out of the blue, and said, "Do you believe in this karma thing?" Intrigued, I asked, "Why, what's going on?" She then proceeded to share with me the details of her new promotion. Having lost out on the "break-through-the-glass-ceiling" opportunity, she had been put into running for another senior-level responsibility, and she'd won that promotion. It was a better job—lots of responsibility and opportunity, and better career benefits. It also was a much better fit for her family, her relationships, and her personal responsibilities.

The story continues. Less than a year later, the original position that she had lost out on by living her values was eliminated. Her new position continues to this day.

The day she lost that first promotion, I asked her how she felt. I was expecting her to dwell on her disappointment, her sense of loss, her "what if" scenarios. There had been some of that, but what else she shared has stayed with me to this day.

She didn't use the term *inner peace*, but that's what she meant. She talked about how she felt she'd done the right thing in keeping the confidence and how, if that had cost her the job, it was worth it. You see, there's always a reward, even when the one you're seeking gets taken away. And often that other reward is what we call inner peace—the moment when the gap between what you truly value and the choice you make in the moment closes and you know that, whatever comes next, you did the right thing.

A Woman's Value

As a woman who works with, counsels, and teaches women every day, I know certain things about women, things that have been solidified through my interactions with medical professionals. As a general rule, women struggle with a higher risk for depression because they can't or won't let things go. Holding on to something can become a problem because, in not letting it go, we focus on that thing—whatever it is. And whatever we focus on and think about most becomes the strongest thing in our lives—for good or for ill.

Every day I teach women that instead of focusing on things that have happened, that didn't work out, that weren't fair or right, they should put their energy into the primary value of simply doing their best. I help them clarify that value with this additional insight: Your best is enough." I remind them that they need role models and, especially when I am talking to girls or young women (who may be a little more focused on their outside role models rather than their inner person), I remind them, "You don't want to wear her shoes; you want to wear her walk."

All of us, women and men, need to let go, to stop giving value to things that are destructive to inner peace and to quality of life. We need to focus on the values that move us forward and lift us up. And once we're back on that upward track, we need to add one more element to our values—a concern for and a dedication to lifting others. The way I say it is, "When you've moved up, you reach back and lift the next person up."

Dr. Martin Luther King Jr. said, "Injustice anywhere is a threat to justice everywhere." When we don't live our values, move forward and upward, we create injustice in our own lives. And, in not living our values and moving forward, we prevent ourselves from being in a place where we can reach out and lift others—and that only spreads the injustice.

On the other hand, when we let go, focus on our values, and move upward, we free ourselves to lift others and the injustice gives way to justice, fear gives way to hope, and a terrible past is replaced with a bright, shining future.

This movement starts in our personal choices, in our homes and families. It can then spread to our communities, our country, and our world. When we individually choose to live our lives like ripples in the great pond of life, they spread. And as they spread they lift others.

If each one of us would commit to closing the gaps between what we value and how we live our lives, we'd start to feel inner peace, and in that moment of inspiration we'd start to help others live their values and close the gaps in their lives. It's the old "pay it forward" idea, like paying the toll on the interstate for the car behind you. When you take the higher path, you set the example and provide the opportunity and the challenge for others to do the right thing, to live their values and begin the process of closing the gaps in their lives.

Purposeful living, rooted in your real values, will change you and make you a better person—for yourself and for everyone around you. I've been doing this—better and better each year—since, as a little girl, I learned to rejoice in the fact that my brother was getting a new coat.

Think about Indiana Jones again. For the Values Gap, the cave across the chasm represents your governing values, the highest priorities in your life. The ledge where you stand represents what you actually do. When what you do closes in on what you value most, you experience inner peace.

> When your daily activities are in concert with
> your highest priorities, you have a credible
> claim to inner peace.

CHAPTER 3

The Time Gap

Closing the Time Gap

In the many seminars and speeches that I have given about living more effectively, people often say, almost wistfully, "I wish I had lived a hundred years ago, when they had more time."

My response to that is, "Really? How much more time did they have a hundred years ago?"

And the response is usually something like "Well . . . they had a whole lot more time."

Reflecting on that widespread desire for more time, I have come to realize that when it comes to time, the only difference between now and a hundred years ago is that we have more options in how we use our time. We have more options because we can do things faster. With modern household appliances, for example, what took a few days to do a hundred years ago can now be done in three hours on Monday morning. Instead of taking two or three hours to prepare dinner, we can now do it in twenty minutes.

A hundred years ago, advances in technology had already shortened the time needed to cross North America from three months in a stagecoach or wagon train to less than a week on a railway train. Today, we can go from New York to San Francisco in four and a half hours, eating dinner and watching a movie as we fly across the continent at nearly six hundred miles per hour.

What was once the standard mode for long distance correspondence is now called snail mail. We can communicate with anyone anywhere in the world via text messaging, e-mail, or Skype instantaneously. The speed at which computers function is accelerating at a seemingly lightning-fast pace. In fact, today's society demands speed in everything.

One seminar participant told me, "I feel like I'm in a pressure cooker. When you pull a miracle out of the hat one day, it becomes expected performance the next day. There are days when I feel as though I've spent all my time meeting everybody else's needs except my own."

In the past, when the pressures got too great, we could escape to a quiet place or leave the office and bask in the silence and privacy of the drive home. Not these days. Our communications technology goes with us everywhere we go. Mobile devices make the car just an extension of the office as we conduct business, solve problems, check out leads, check in with our broker, get the shopping lists for the market, and otherwise continue the unrelenting stress.

But the fact remains, with all the changes that have happened in our lifetime—whether we're "boomers,"

"Gen Xers," "Millennials," or whatever comes next—one thing has never changed nor will it ever change, and that is the amount of time we all have.

Hectic as the days of our lives may seem, we all have the same daily allotment of twenty-four hours that our ancestors had. There have always been seven days in the week, and twenty-four hours in the day, whether it is 1400 BC, AD 1400, or today. What has changed is the amount of stuff we're trying to cram into those same hours. Freed from the daily struggle just to exist, we can let our time be filled with meaningless activity and motion or choose to spend it doing the things that matter most to us.

This choice is the root of the third gap—the Time Gap (or, as it is sometimes called, the Productivity Gap). This is the gap between what we want to do with our time and how we actually spend it. Making the best choices and closing the Time Gap requires understanding three principles:

1. the concept of event control
2. the power of daily planning
3. the discipline of managing your planning

When you acquire and apply these three productivity principles you'll start to close the gap between where you *want* to spend your time and where you *are* actually spending it.

Event Control

I've started hundreds and hundreds of seminars by asking someone in the audience to define time. I usually get a blank stare, and then get such responses as, "it's money," "it's the clock," "it's the hours in a day," and so on. None of those responses are accurate. Albert Einstein's definition of time was

> Time is the occurrence of events in sequence
> one after the other.

Everything is an event: walking into a room, getting out of bed in the morning, brushing your teeth, driving to work. Time is the occurrence of all these events in sequence, one after the other. When I was teaching at Merrill Lynch, a fellow handed me a three-by-five card that read, "Time is what keeps one darn thing after another from becoming every darn thing at once."

Management, according to many dictionary definitions, involves the act of controlling. So what is time management?

The Act of Controlling Events

The question now becomes, What are the events over which I have any control? Let me introduce you to the Control Model.

The left side of this model represents events over which you have no control. The right side represents events over which you have total control. And the middle represents everything else—the things over which you have varying amounts of control.

Consider the left side of the model for a moment. What are the events over which you have no control? Weather, death, taxes, and traffic, to name a few. Think about the feelings that you experience when you are up against the left side: frustration, stress, anxiety, maybe even some depression. The feelings that you likely have on this side are not pleasant. The bottom line is, when you are out of control, you probably don't feel very good.

I had a fun experience a long time ago with my first time on a ski lift. My wife and I went skiing without bothering to get lessons; we just got on a lift. Halfway up the mountain, I realized that the seats were coming back the other way empty. I asked my wife, "How do you get off the lift?" She just looked at me and didn't bother to answer. I soon discovered that the only way off the lift was to ski off. I wish I had a video of my first exit from the lift; it was not a controlled experience. I experienced all of the feelings I have described above with one addition: pain. It doesn't feel good to be out of control.

Now, move slowly across the model from left to right. The right side represents total control. Think about some events over which you have total control: the time you get up, what you wear, how you might react to somebody else's attitude or choices, what you eat, and so forth. Notice that all of these things have one focus in common: *you*. The only thing you have 100 percent control over is you; everything else falls under either the partial control or no control categories.

Using the control model to categorize events, you can choose your response to the situations you encounter. People who master event control begin the process of closing the Time Gap in their lives. They put their time to better use and the gap between what they want to do with their time and how they actually spend that time starts to close.

The closer we get to being in control of what can be controlled, the more likely we are to experience inner peace.

Once you understand the concept of event control then you're ready to start daily planning.

Daily Planning

Daily planning is the key to managing the events over which we have total control. Think about the last ten days, and ask yourself this question: How many minutes each day did I spend formally planning that day?

Shower time doesn't count. Neither does driving or exercise time, even though these moments might be wonderful times to think. I'm talking about formal planning time where you sit down and consider not only the day's activities but also your values and priorities in relation to the day's activities.

Although there are only twenty-four hours in a day, time can be leveraged. Investing a little of your time in daily planning can actually free up time throughout the rest of the day. A daily planning session can act as a time lever. The cost is small—only ten to fifteen minutes per day—but you will enjoy the benefits all day long, such as clearly defined tasks with deadlines, increased focus on more important tasks, less time spent between projects, and a greater sense of accomplishment at the end of the day. Aren't those outcomes worth a few dedicated minutes of your time?

Edwin C. Bliss, author of *Getting Things Done*, has said, "The more time we spend on planning a project, the less total time is required for it. Don't let today's busywork crowd planning time out of your schedule."

In a previous book, *The 10 Natural Laws of Successful Time and Life Management*, I introduced the principle of the *magic three hours*, which in theory is a generally uninterrupted block of time that can be used to get your day on track both physically and emotionally. It might be late at night, early in the morning, or some other block of time when you prepare for your day. Some magic three-hour activities might include physical exercise or studying a personal core book, and it should include at least fifteen minutes planning your day.

Since the writing of that book, the pace of life has sped up, and I realize that finding a literal three hours of uninterrupted time to get the day on track is not always realistic. But there is not one of us that can't find fifteen minutes to plan. The act of planning is an event over which we have total control. So I now refer to the daily planning commitment as the *magic fifteen minutes*.

Those fifteen minutes, carefully invested at the beginning of every day, will close the gap—*every day*—between what you want to get done and what you actually do.

Those fifteen minutes can create magic in your life, and the following seven steps will help you do just that.

> **Step 1: Find a Quiet Place.** You need fifteen minutes of real focus. Find the right place—one where you won't be interrupted by other people, e-mail, phone calls, texts, tweets, and the like.
>
> **Step 2: Seek Inspiration.** Take a moment to seek inspiration through meditation, prayer, or whatever source through which you normally find inspiration.
>
> **Step 3: Review Your Values.** In chapter 2, you built your values as part of closing the Values Gap. These governing values are the core of your life, and they need to be manifested in your day.
>
> **Step 4: Integrate Your Long-Range Goals.** Make sure that the things you are planning for the long term also show up in what you're planning for the short term.
>
> **Step 5: List Your Appointments.** Every life, every job, every day has appointments. These are simply events that are "time-fixed"—they have to happen at a specific time. Identify and record these activities.
>
> **Step 6: List Your Tasks.** Tasks, which often end up on "to-do" lists, are "time flexible"—they can be done at any time as long as they eventually get done. Make sure the number of tasks and the amount of time required for each is well within the time available in your day. Many of us have a tendency

to overplan our days; consequently, we can feel defeated by our plan before we even begin, or discouraged at the end of the day because we haven't made a dent in our list.

Step 7: Prioritize Your Tasks. This final key is vital. Even the best plans can run aground. Unforeseen events can leave us far from the end of our task list at the end of the day. But if we've started with those tasks that are most important, we can have the satisfaction of knowing that whatever we've left undone is less critical than what we've accomplished.

That's it—fifteen minutes and seven steps to create your plan for the day.

Managing the Unexpected

Sometimes, despite your best planning efforts, unexpected things can come up that completely throw off your original plan for the day. In fact, interruptions and unforeseen events consume much of our time in the twenty-first century because they can reach out and find us anywhere. As never before in history, social media, e-mail, texts, phone calls, and the like can bring the unexpected to us twenty-four hours a day.

Unexpected events in and of themselves are neither good nor bad; they just exist. But so does the plan that you created during your magic fifteen minutes. When an unexpected event pops up, you have a choice between putting off the unexpected and sticking with your plan, or altering the plan to deal with whatever has come up.

Some unforeseen events require you to respond to them immediately, such as a medical emergency or the immediate needs of young children. Other unexpected demands on your time come with a choice to deal or not deal with them immediately.

For example, a coworker comes into your office and says, "Hey, I need fifteen minutes of your time on this project," but you are currently working on a presentation for your boss. You could choose to say, "You know what? I can't do that right now. Come back in an hour, and I can help you then." That unexpected demand on your time was trumped by your predetermined plan to prepare a presentation for your boss during that particular hour.

It is very important to make the distinction between unexpected demands on your time that do not have to be dealt with immediately and those that require you to drop everything. What you choose to do in that moment will either widen the Time Gap or narrow it.

So how can you know when to stick with the plan and when to deviate from it? The best choice grows out of knowing what you're trying to achieve in advance.

Consider the concept of *opportunity cost* for just a moment. If I gave you ten thousand dollars and told you it had to be spent in the next four hours, what would you spend it on? Let's say you decide to put that money toward buying a car. The minute you decide to spend it on a car, what have you decided *not* to spend the money on? Everything else. So the opportunity cost of the car is something else you could have spent the money on.

All Time Is the Same

The minute you decide to spend one hour watching TV, by virtue of that decision, what have you decided *not* to spend the hour on? Everything else!

When you're presented with an "in the moment" conflict between what you planned to do and what has unexpectedly come up, choose the action most in concert with your governing values; rarely will it be the wrong decision, and your personal constitution will suddenly become a living document.

To get to this point, you may have to rewrite some principles on your Belief Window when it comes to what you do in your precious twenty-four hours. Here is a belief to consider writing on your window:

> When confronted with unforeseen events, the best option will always be in concert with my governing values and best meet my needs over time.

Keep in mind that there are two fallacies of time that we are tempted to believe:

1. We think we can get more of it.
2. We think we can save it somehow.

Are either true? No. When you hear someone say, "I don't have time," he or she is not telling you the truth. We all have all the time there is. What they are really saying is something quite different. For example, if someone asked me to go to lunch and my response was, "I don't have time," I'm not telling the truth. What I'm really saying is, "I value some other event more."

Closing the Time Gap

We have now discussed the Time Gap, which involves getting what we most care about done in the twenty-four hours a day that we have. Take control of how you confront the events in your life. Invest the magic fifteen minutes every day and follow the seven steps of daily planning outlined above.

Finally, learn to evaluate the opportunity cost of the choices you make in your life. Balance the unexpected with what you've already planned by making choices that center on your governing values, meet your needs over time, and bring inner peace.

If you are truly serious about closing the Time Gap, make the commitment to spend a magic fifteen minutes planning every single day.

McKay Christensen

McKay Christensen and I go back many years. He is the president of a multibillion-dollar, fast-growing, global company. He is highly respected by everyone he works with and by clients all over the world. His ability to close the Time Gap has resulted in a remarkable company. The hallmark of his success is his natural humility. Here is his story.

(McKay) As a teenager I worked for a kind, generous man who owned several farms. On one of his farms, we grew sod, which was cut, stacked on pallets, and shipped to surrounding cities where new businesses and homeowners would acquire the sod and an instant, green lawn.

Typically we would plant the sod in late fall and harvest it the following summer. We used a self-contained sod harvester to dig it up, along with a one-inch layer of dirt that would keep the sod intact. The harvester then conveyed the sod to a blade, which would cut it into three-foot strips and then drop the strips down to the two workers standing on the back of the machine, who would stack the strips of sod onto a pallet. The harvester weighed about fourteen tons; the driver sat in the front, the engine sat directly behind him, and the workers stacking the sod stood on a platform above the rear wheels.

On July 5, 1987, I was assigned to work with my high school classmate on the back of the harvester while another friend drove it. Another followed behind with a forklift to carry away the pallets of sod as we released them from the back of the harvester.

We were moving the harvester from one end of the field, across a section of hard, dry dirt, to another part of the farm. The machine ran at three to five miles per hour. I was walking beside the harvester while my friend and I talked about the events of the previous day.

I attempted to jump up onto the platform to sit next to my friend, but I misjudged, landing only part way onto the platform. As I lost my balance, I fell in the path of the double set of dual wheels underneath the platform.

I immediately tried to scurry out of the path of the wheels, but my high-top sneakers got caught by the big knobby tires, which started to roll up my leg, throwing me to the ground. I quickly realized I was in major trouble; I was lying feet-first directly in the path of the four wheels. I strained to lean forward onto my right side to keep my head out of the path of the machine.

I felt my left leg break under the immense weight. As I turned to my side, the wheels climbed onto my pelvis, which crumbled grotesquely. I had never felt anything so excruciatingly painful in all my life. My back and ribs were the next to snap as the wheels climbed up my stomach and chest. Then the machine mercilessly twisted me onto my back, with the knobby treads running over my shoulder and the side of my face and neck. Miraculously, the machine missed most of my head, not crushing my skull, which would have meant an instant death.

By the time the slow-rolling wheels had finished their devastating work, I had lost consciousness. The first thing I remember when I opened my eyes was the inconceivable pain and a feeling like I was underwater. I was trying to breathe, but it wasn't working the way it was supposed to. I started to panic. I couldn't speak; I couldn't cry out for help, even though I frantically wanted to. Everything hurt so badly. I quickly grasped the fact that I was about to die, and the pain was so extreme that I wanted to die. I just wanted it to stop.

I later learned that I suffered from a *pneumothorax*—in simple terms, my lungs had collapsed. When a healthy person breathes, he or she uses the chest muscles to expand the chest, allowing the lungs to inflate, similar to a balloon. During exhalation those muscles relax, releasing the air. If there is a puncture in the lung tissue due to trauma, the air escapes to the area outside of the lungs yet inside the chest cavity. As a result, the lungs push together like a wet paper sack, and the air inside the chest cavity is unable to escape. This pressure keeps the lungs from expanding and can lead to cardiac arrest or respiratory failure.

Both of my lungs had collapsed, and everything in my body was screaming for oxygen. My brain, heart, lungs—everything was suffocating. And in my desperation to breathe, I had to move to expand my chest cavity to allow even a small part of my lungs to gather air. This meant I had to move my broken ribs and back. The pain of even the slightest movement was almost more than I could endure, but it was the only way to get even the smallest relief of more air.

The farm manager, a kind man named Stan whom I admired a great deal, had arrived out of breath. He could sense I was deep in shock and on the edge of giving up entirely. He took my head in his hands and spoke to me. For whatever reason, his kind and reassuring words reached through the panic and pain. He told me I was strong; he gave me the thought that I was going to live, something that before that moment had never entered my mind. Until that moment I had only wondered how long the pain would continue until I could die and make it go away: when would I stop breathing all together?

But Stan spoke belief into me; I started to believe that I could live. Although this thought was at first incomprehensible, it started to work into my thinking. "McKay, you're going to live," he told me, and he started telling me of the great things that I would do in life.

It was more than fifteen minutes, which seemed like fifteen years, before the ambulance arrived. I was so broken that they didn't know how to safely get me off the ground and onto the gurney. The minute they rolled me one direction or the other, I screamed in pain, but they soon figured how to do it despite my protests. The doctors quickly ordered the insertion of a chest tube, which meant they cut through my chest cavity in between my ribs and inserted a tube to evacuate the excess air. It hurt so badly I couldn't cope, but soon thereafter the pain in my chest diminished, and I could breathe a little bit better.

It took almost a year for me to heal. Much of that time I spent flat on my back in bed. I learned a lot about myself, about life, and about what's most important. I am sure others who have come within a whisper of death feel the same: life is a gift, not to be wasted or squandered. I try my best to remember that fact. And when I treat my life as a gift, I find I can do hard things.

Later in life, as an adult, I made up my mind that I wanted to do two things. First, I wanted to teach, to share the insights my life had given me with others. I specifically wanted to teach in an academic environment, at a prestigious university. I wanted to have a platform—not one that would feed my ego but one that would support my message.

The second thing I wanted to do was make a difference. Stan's love and concern as he held me in my moment of greatest need, and his belief that I would live to do important things, never left me. I didn't know what those important things were, but I believed Stan. God had things for me to do.

Having been within minutes of knowing that my time on this earth was almost up, I gained a deep and profound respect for time. Time is something I teach about a lot. It's something my students struggle with and have a lot of questions about. They're learning for the first time in their lives that they have more to do than they have time for. They're rapidly waking up to the fact that the way that they've been living, the way that they've been organizing their time, will no longer do.

When their grades slip a bit, when they get married while they're still in school, as they try to support themselves or a family for the first time, when they reach the point in life that their parents are no longer supporting them, or when they're trying to prepare for graduate school, they all of a sudden have more to handle than they think they can possibly manage.

I've learned that one of the secrets to getting our time back—in many ways, getting our precious lives back—lies in moving beyond the embedded bad habits into the discipline of good ones and persisting long enough to see the difference that can make.

Putting off the things that I like to do is uncomfortable, but when I stay engaged in that process for a period of time, it becomes normal to me. It becomes a good feeling, and the peace comes when I begin to exercise the good habits. The feeling of self-worth and authorship that comes from this discipline is intoxicating. Most of us have lived a life in which we feel like we're subject to someone else's script.

When I procrastinate, I'm subjected to my mood, or I'm subjected to the impulses that come to me from other people. I'm subjected to the negative feelings or self-talk that I bring upon myself. But when I start to do what I know I should and exercise confidence toward doing what I said I would do the moment I said I'd do it, I get a feeling of authorship—that I'm writing my own script.

I've experienced it in my own life. The reason it feels good is because now, all of a sudden, I've aligned my activity and my mood with my goals. I believe this ability is God-given; I believe that we can feel more at ease in our lives when we have shifted this alignment.

When I was lying on my back, with nearly every bone in my body crushed and feeling unimaginable pain, I gained a perspective on what really matters in life. In that first fifteen minutes as I lay there waiting for help, I gained an insight into how simple my real priorities in life are—to live without pain, to be loved, to breathe.

And yet I, like most of us, continually find myself in the trap of wasting my time on things that don't really matter.

In addition to my work at the university, I work at a company where we do 360-degree performance reviews. The first time that these reviews came around, the direct reports told me exactly what working for me was like. It was horrible: "We can't rely on you. We can't trust you. You don't think anything's important. You don't show up for meetings. You don't follow up on the assignments that you gave me, so I guess I'm not important. I don't really need to do them. I don't need to be prepared for the meeting when we show up." People can't lead that way; it's impossible to lead that way.

I had to take a step back, and in doing so I learned a great lesson about prioritization and time. I asked myself a simple question in regard to each direct report or each major area of responsibility that I had: What one thing could I do that would make everything else easier in my day-to-day activities and in the responsibilities that I have? And an answer came to me.

I found that prioritizing what was most important, and being willing to say no, consistently made managing easier. When I got really clear about what I was going to do and what I was not going to do, and then set the expectations accordingly, I suddenly started to be able to stick to my schedule, to meet expectations, and to make it to the meetings I said I would attend.

Maybe my answer is good for everybody, or maybe it is just good for me, but the question is still the same: What one thing could you do to make all other things easier? The answer will help you to prioritize and to move forward in a much more effective way.

About five years ago I was into my career big time. I was president of a company that was expanding internationally; I was on the road. I had thirteen direct reports at the time, and it was way too many. We were in the middle of a big transition at work, and I was failing at home.

I wasn't simply not keeping up; I was failing significantly. I returned to this question: What one thing could I do? My marriage was failing not only because of time but also because of how I was when I was around my wife: tired and stressed. I'm not really an outgoing, verbal person, and I was failing to give her what she needed at that time in her life.

When I asked myself what one thing I could do to make everything else easier in my marriage, I knew what the answer was: I needed to be a person who was vocal about how I felt about her and about the good things that she was doing. It was really pretty easy, except when I was tired or when I was not in the mood. But I said to myself, Look, I'm going to spend just a few minutes every day, when I have the opportunity, to let her know what she does well, to let her know what is so good about her.

It was amazing. Even with just the few minutes of exercising that one action, all of the things in my marriage became easier. My wife's feelings for me changed; she responded to me, and we interacted in an entirely different way. It only took mentioning the small things—complimenting her on the way she did normal, everyday activities; recognizing her talents; being positive in my language about her. It didn't come naturally to me, but it made all the difference; all the other things in our marriage started to become much easier.

So asking that question—What one thing could I do to make everything easier?—helps to prioritize; the answer finds the one most leveraged action. It really works.

At that same time in my life, I was failing with my kids. I'll tell you the story exactly as it was. I was horrible; I wasn't just bad, I was *horrible*.

I had two kids in junior high, one in high school, and one in elementary school. I had a busy household and a busy work schedule, and I was failing. Often when I came home from work, the first things I saw were shoes on the floor, things lying around, jobs that my son was supposed to do that he hadn't done; all the household things that I expected the kids to take care of weren't done. And I would just let them have it. I wouldn't yell and scream, but the first thing that they heard from me was, "You need to do this. Why didn't you do it? I told you to do this. Give me your cell phone until you can get this done." It became a habit that I just fell into.

I was judging and criticizing all the time. I had no relationship with my kids. They didn't come to me voluntarily, and there wasn't any positive language in what was going on in our household. I was really struggling.

I was reading the Scriptures one day, and I read, "God created the sun and the moon and the stars and all of the planets. He did that and put them in proximity of each other so that they could give light to each other." *He put the stars and planets in their close paths, so that they could give light to each other!*

All of a sudden I realized that the Scriptures compare us to those planets. It occurred to me that I had been placed in the path I was in to give light to my children; they were put in proximity to me. We were in the same orbit, the same household, so that I could give light to them. I decided from that point forward that I was going to change from being a critic and a judge to being a light and a help. I even had a sign painted on top of my office door to remind me to be a light and not a judge.

And I started. It was hard. On my way home from work I knew I was going to fall into the old habit, so I would sit in the garage after I arrived home and tell myself, "When you walk in the house you have to step over the backpacks. You have to go past the shoes. You have to go past this and you just have to just ask the kids how their day was. You have to tell your daughters they look nice. Give a compliment. When one of the children has something to talk about, just be quiet. Even though you're tired and want to go into your cave, just sit and listen to them if they want to talk."

I started doing that. It was hard at first, and it felt out of character. And you know what? Things started to change. My kids started to come to me for guidance. I had more and more opportunity to ask, and to guide, and to coach them at the appropriate times rather than to be just a judge and a critic. You should see what returned to our household: peace and faith, and trust in each other, became normal. It was awesome!

I learned that as parents we need to remember that sometimes our mood can dictate the mood of the household. Remembering that enabled me to do what Hyrum talks about a lot, which is to exercise control in the moment and live according to my values. It made a huge difference in my family.

Every day I spend fifteen minutes of dedicated planning time. I will tell you: setting aside the time is hard to do at first. To be able to be fully engaged, to be fully centered in that activity for that fifteen-minute period, to get into it quickly and out of it quickly without interruption, is a habit that takes practice. But it's a talent that anyone can develop.

This talent relies on the concept of full engagement. When people are fully engaged in an activity, they do it more effectively, with more depth, concentration, and intent. The habit begins to establish itself during the fifteen minutes in the morning, then extends into all areas of life. People who develop this talent are more apt to jump into the deep things, the serious matters; they will be more candid when they should be, more constructive, prepared, open, and coachable. All of these great characteristics surface when a person is operating in a fully engaged manner, centered at the deep level of any activity.

Getting distracted is so easy. Just taking a quick look at e-mail can send me off the track, down seemingly endless chains of messages. It is just too disruptive, so I try to never look at my e-mail in the morning. Instead, I get up and begin my fifteen minutes by reading the Scriptures. I recognize that what I might consider inspirational may not be the same for everyone, but I strongly believe that starting my daily planning with something inspirational—the Scriptures, affirmation, meditation, prayer, contemplation, inspired readings—is key to my successfully engaging in the whole day. The inspirational reading reminds me what's most important when I plan, and I have found that the planning works very, very quickly that way.

Stephen Covey describes an "educated conscience." By confidently feeding a conscience with the values that are important to you, and reinforcing those values through good, uplifting reading and through discussions with good people: through a daily appetite of those things we strengthen our ability to choose integrity when the moment of choice comes. We can do what we say we will do and can follow through on things we know we should follow through on; we can be completely honest with ourselves and others and can do hard things, such as apologizing when we need to. An educated conscience does that work for us; it can give promptings, such as ideas or feelings during the fifteen minutes of daily planning.

I believe there's a link between a highly educated conscience and someone who consistently thinks about and decides what to do each day based on their personal values. Someone who acts on those values will experience more in their life.

Achieving Goals

Fundamentally, the discipline of overcoming challenges, pursuing goals, planning, and being fully present in the things I do have brought great blessings to my life. Underlying much of what I've done and giving energy to it are my two original goals— to teach in an academic environment and to make a real difference in the world.

I have spent my adult life focused on these principles—understanding them, expanding them based on my own experience, and working diligently to make them a living part of my life. As a result, a lot has changed. I've sometimes gotten things wrong, such as how I originally dealt with my children when arriving home from a stressful day's work. And I've gotten a lot of things right.

I completed my doctorate in 1997, focusing my dissertation on the eight stages of development people pass through in their adult lives. I learned two things from my research: reading really matters to growth and maturity, and working with a more experienced mentor helps us to learn to deal with the reality of our lives. This reminds me very much of what Hyrum teaches in the Reality Model and the Belief Window.

My doctorate was elemental to the opportunity to join the faculty at the Marriott School of Management at Brigham Young University, where I teach MBA students some of these fundamental skills.

I have had many opportunities to make a difference. Central to the pursuit and achievement of that goal has been the establishing of the website www.openyoureyes.org. My partner and dear friend, Jake Olson, and I focus every day on helping people "live with faith and find the winner within." Jake's battle managing a rare form of cancer that took his sight, thus ending his lifelong goal of playing football, inspires me every day with a real sense of the power we all possess to make choices in life regardless of our circumstances. And then, through planning and perseverance, we can see our goals and aspirations come to fruition.

Reflect on Indiana Jones one last time. For the Time Gap, the cave across the chasm represents what you plan to do today, and the ledge represents what you will actually do. Inner peace and a dramatic increase in your ability to make a difference occurs when you move what you do in line with what you plan to do.

Conclusion

Now you know what the Three Gaps are: the Beliefs Gap, the Values Gap, and the Time Gap. You've read three compelling stories about people who have closed their own gaps, and you have been given a simple methodology for how to close these gaps in your own life. The question now is, Are you going to do anything about this?

Let me share my definition of *character* with you. This is not a dictionary definition, but *my* definition.

> Character is the ability to carry out a worthy decision after the emotion of making that decision has passed.

Many years ago, at work, I had a ritual every morning at 9:30 a.m.: I would go into our company lunchroom and pay homage to a shrine. The shrine was a candy bar vending machine. I would put a quarter into that little slot and retrieve a Heath Bar. To say I was addicted to Heath Bars would not have been much of an exaggeration.

On one occasion, as I was about to get my daily fix of chocolate, two people sitting across the room, obviously thinking that I couldn't hear them, said to each other, "Hyrum is getting porky, isn't he?"

My hand froze in midair; I put the quarter back in my pocket and stormed out of the lunchroom. At that point in my life, I weighed 230 pounds, which was forty pounds too many for me. My wife had been at me for two years to lose the weight; I picked up the phone, called her, and said *this time* I was going to lose the weight. I was emotionally involved. How long do you think that commitment lasted? Four hours.

What happens in four hours when you've made a commitment like that? You get hungry, that's what happens. And you find yourself leaning on the third shelf of your refrigerator, eating everything you can get your hands on.

> *Character,* simply stated, is doing what
> you say you're going to do.

I learned long ago that an excellent definition of the term *wisdom* is "knowledge rightly applied." You have gained some knowledge inside the pages of this book—knowledge that comes from many wonderful places. The question now becomes, Do you have the character to do anything about it?

There are three things that I would ask you to seriously consider that will stimulate your commitment to start closing the Three Gaps:

1. Write down the things that connected with you.
2. Think about those things for thirty-six hours.
3. Teach those things to somebody else within forty-eight hours after that.

Now start your journey. Close the gaps. Begin your quest for inner peace.

Make a difference.

The Author's Personal Constitution

Hyrum Smith's Governing Values

1. **I love God with all my heart, mind, and strength.** As the Scriptures and the prophets have commanded since the beginning, I seek first the Kingdom of God. I exhibit my love for the Lord by living his laws. I pray often, expressing my appreciation and love for all I have. Most of all, I exhibit my love by the life I live and by my untiring effort to serve Him in whatever capacity I am called.

2. **I love my neighbor as myself.** I recognize and accept the fact that all men and women are equal in the sight of God. I never do anything in any way to harm or destroy the self-worth of another human being. As far as I am able, I aid all people in their needs. Charity is my mortal quest—"the ability to separate behavior from the human being." I do not criticize anyone's beliefs. I honor the individual and his or her right to exist, think, feel, and believe the way he or she chooses.

3. **I obey all the commandments of God.** The commandments of God are clear descriptions of the
   natural laws of the universe. When I obey any
   natural law, I have a credible claim to the natural
   consequences of that law. I obey the commandments for two reasons: (1) God asked me to, and
   (2) they work.

4. **I strive to be an outstanding husband and father.**
   I take sufficient, meaningful time with my wife
   and my children to help them with their spiritual,
   intellectual, social, professional, physical, and
   financial needs. I love my wife with care, respect,
   and kindness. I build strong family unity. I build
   self-esteem in my children and help them maxi-
   mize their potential.

5. **I am humble.** The definition of *humility* that
   works for me is "the realization of our depen-
   dence on God." I recognize that everything I
   have, am, and ever will have or be is a direct gift
   from God. Humility is not weakness, merely a
   recognition of my nothingness in the universe.

6. **I honor the memory of my father and mother.** My
   parents gave me life, taught me the basic principles of Christian living, and set marvelous
   examples for me to follow.

7. **I foster intellectual growth.** A man can think no
   deeper than his vocabulary will allow him to.
   I read regularly each day. I select my reading
   from the best books and articles of the day. One
   cannot teach from an empty well.

8. **I am honest in all things.** I am honest with myself first, recognizing that to be honest with my fellow men requires that I first be honest with myself. I listen to my conscience on all decisions. The Golden Rule is a natural law of the universe. It works.

9. **I use excellent speech.** The ability to communicate orally is a gift. I never use profanity. I use the best English and grammar I know. When a concept is served well, people listen and learn.

10. **I maintain a strong and healthy body.** My body is a temple of God that houses my spirit. Maintaining my governing values is not possible without being in excellent shape. I eat, sleep, and exercise in such a manner as to maintain a high level of energy. I take nothing into my body that will in any way detract from my ability to perform at my peak on a consistent basis. I eliminate negative energy.

11. **I value my time.** A natural by-product of high self-esteem is an increase in the value of time. Managing time is nothing more than gaining control of the events in my life. In a period of solitude every day, I evaluate the events of my life for that day. In this period of introspection, I determine the sequence of events that will have the greatest value to me. Inner peace can come only when I manage what I do according to my governing values.

12. **I am financially independent.** I have developed an income that will be present whether I am capable of working or not. My family's needs are taken care of in such a way that they will never be without food, shelter, transportation, or education.

13. **I have a period of solitude daily.** During this period, I teach my family, read, develop my plan for the day, spend time in prayer both personally and with my family. This experience is brings on inner peace for each day.

14. **I change people's lives.** I teach correct principles and do so in such a way that people will be motivated to experiment with and utilize them. Once these principles are internalized, people will govern themselves in a manner that will bring greater control and inner peace.

15. **I listen well.** I listen carefully to all input, both positive and negative; I weigh it, and then respond with respect and love.

16. **I have order in my life at all times.** I maintain a sense of order in all aspects of my life. My physical surroundings are always clean, organized, and structured so that they bring calm into my life. My personal hygiene is immaculate, as are my personal habits.

About the Author

Hyrum W. Smith is a distinguished author, speaker, businessman, and one of the original creators of the popular Franklin Day Planner. In 1983 he cofounded the Franklin Quest Company to produce the planner and train individuals and organizations in the time-management principles on which the planner was based; in 1997 it became the Franklin Covey Company. Hyrum stepped down as chairman and CEO in 1999; he continued as vice chairman of the company's board until 2004.

For four decades, Hyrum has been empowering people to effectively govern their personal and professional lives. His books and presentations have been acclaimed by American and international audiences. He combines

wit and enthusiasm with a gift for communicating compelling principles that incite lasting personal change.

Hyrum is the author of several nationally acclaimed
books, including *The 10 Natural Laws of Successful Time
and Life Management, What Matters Most, The Modern
Gladiator,* and *You Are What You Believe.*

Hyrum grew up in Honolulu, Hawaii, and spent two
years in London. When he returned from London, he
was drafted into the US Army. He was married in 1966
to Gail Cooper while on leave. They have had six children (five still living) and twenty-four grandchildren
(twenty-two still living).

As an honor graduate from the Officers Candidate
School in Fort Sill, Oklahoma, Hyrum commanded a
Pershing missile unit in Germany. He graduated from
Brigham Young University in 1971 with a degree in busi-
ness management.

Hyrum has received numerous honors and community
service awards, including the following:

- International Entrepreneur of the Year, from
  Brigham Young University's Marriott School
  of Management, 1993.
- Three honorary doctorate degrees.
- SRI Gallup Hall of Fame and Man of the Year
  Award, 1992.
- Silver Beaver Award from the Boy Scouts of
  America, 1986.
- Induction into the Utah Business Hall of Fame,
  2000.

Hyrum enjoys golfing, shooting pistols and rifles, listening to classical music, horse riding, and spending time with his family at his ranch in southern Utah.

He has recently founded a new business called 3 Gaps.

Contributing Authors

Jennifer and Tyler Wilkinson

Jennifer Orton Wilkinson is the daughter of Ray and Dorothy Orton. She grew up in St. George, Utah, where she developed a wonderful friendship with her future husband Tyler Wilkinson during middle and high school. Jennifer attended  Dixie State College, where she danced as a Rebelette and was voted copresident by her teammates. She has great appreciation for her experiences at Dixie, where she graduated with an associate of science degree. In 1994 she married Tyler in the St. George Latter Day Saints temple, and they now have five beautiful, smart, and especially *perfect* children.

Jennifer loves raising children and has developed a true appreciation for being a stay-at-home mom. She loves home life, traveling, and anything that involves her husband and children—even camping.

Tyler Wilkinson grew up in St. George, Utah, where he attended Dixie High School and garnered all-state honors in football and baseball and won the 3A wrestling championship in his weight class. There he also met and began dating his future wife, Jennifer Orton. During the spring of his senior year, shortly after signing a letter of intent to play both college football and baseball, Tyler broke his neck in an automobile accident, leaving him a quadriplegic.

Following his accident, Tyler earned his associates degree and graduated from Dixie Junior College. He then completed his bachelor's degree at Southern Utah University, where he graduated summa cum laude and was recognized as the university's Most Outstanding Business Student.

While attending college, Tyler continued to date Jennifer and they were married in the spring of 1994. Events of Tyler and Jennifer's lives are told by National Football League Hall of Fame quarterback Steve Young in the film *Tyler: A Real Hero*. The film has been aired both nationally and internationally and has resulted in Tyler sharing his message of faith and perseverance more than a thousand times with professional, civic, and church organizations around the world.

Tyler lives in St. George, where he is a partner and vice president in the firm Soltis Investment Advisors. He and Jennifer have been married for twenty-one years and they have five wonderful children.

Linda Clemons

Linda Clemons, the CEO of Sisterpreneur, Inc., is a global speaker and expert in sales and nonverbal communication ("body language"). She teaches women, men, and corporate clients the strategies to communicate and persuade more effectively by learning to "see the invisible and hear the inaudible."

Linda's personal values are her set of beliefs and ethical guidelines that have allowed her to gain clarity about what she stands for. They have played a tremendous role in her happiness, success, and, most important, inner peace. These personal values have allowed her to interact harmoniously with those who share them.

McKay Christensen

McKay Christensen is the president of Melaleuca, a $1.2 billion consumer products company with hundreds of thousands of employees and marketing executives. In that role McKay speaks to audiences around the world about leadership, teamwork, perseverance, and personal performance. In his current position and his past leadership roles with Fortune 500 companies, he has led diverse teams in marketing, sales, and management.

McKay has written numerous articles on career development, leadership, and business management and has coauthored a book on career development. He has an MBA and a PhD in organization and adult learning.

As part of his doctoral work, McKay led groundbreaking research on how adults learn and find happiness. This research, one of the most comprehensive quantitative studies of its kind, reveals how people can learn to be happy. His research and publication experience includes topics such as servant leadership, transformation as adults, and lasting change. McKay has a heartfelt passion for helping others reach their full potential, and he currently teaches strategy management courses at the Marriott School of Management at Brigham Young University.

McKay was born on Luke Air Force Base in Glendale, Arizona, the son of a fighter pilot. He grew up with seven brothers and sisters. Without much money and a lot of mouths to feed, McKay's parents taught their children to work at an early age; whether delivering newspapers, cleaning horse stalls, or working in the local flour mill, hard work was part of everyday life. At the age of fifteen, McKay was run over and crushed by a fourteen-ton harvester in a farming accident that left him with a broken leg and back, a crushed pelvis, two collapsed lungs, and a dozen other broken bones. He spent months recovering.

As a college student McKay learned to speak Japanese, and he has lived and worked in Japan. He is an avid runner who has completed numerous marathons, including the Boston Marathon several times. He learned to fly-fish as a young man living in the Rocky Mountains, and he still loves to escape to the South Fork of the Snake River for a day of fishing.

McKay and his wife Jennifer are the parents of five children.

Berrett–Koehler
BK Publishers

Berrett-Koehler is an independent publisher dedicated to an ambitious mission: *connecting people and ideas to create a world that works for all.*

We believe that to truly create a better world, action is needed at all levels—individual, organizational, and societal. At the individual level, our publications help people align their lives with their values and with their aspirations for a better world. At the organizational level, our publications promote progressive leadership and management practices, socially responsible approaches to business, and humane and effective organizations. At the societal level, our publications advance social and economic justice, shared prosperity, sustainability, and new solutions to national and global issues.

A major theme of our publications is "Opening Up New Space." Berrett-Koehler titles challenge conventional thinking, introduce new ideas, and foster positive change. Their common quest is changing the underlying beliefs, mindsets, institutions, and structures that keep generating the same cycles of problems, no matter who our leaders are or what improvement programs we adopt.

We strive to practice what we preach—to operate our publishing company in line with the ideas in our books. At the core of our approach is stewardship, which we define as a deep sense of responsibility to administer the company for the benefit of all of our "stakeholder" groups: authors, customers, employees, investors, service providers, and the communities and environment around us.

We are grateful to the thousands of readers, authors, and other friends of the company who consider themselves to be part of the "BK Community." We hope that you, too, will join us in our mission.

A BK Life Book

This book is part of our BK Life series. BK Life books change people's lives. They help individuals improve their lives in ways that are beneficial for the families, organizations, communities, nations, and world in which they live and work. To find out more, visit **www.bk-life.com**.

Berrett–Koehler
Publishers

Connecting people and ideas
to create a world that works for all

Dear Reader,

Thank you for picking up this book and joining our worldwide community of Berrett-Koehler readers. We share ideas that bring positive
change into people's lives, organizations, and society.

To welcome you, we'd like to offer you a free e-book. You can pick
from among twelve of our bestselling books by entering the promo-
tional code **BKP92E** here: http://www.bkconnection.com/welcome.

When you claim your free e-book, we'll also send you a copy of our
e-newsletter, the *BK Communiqué*. Although you're free to unsub-
scribe, there are many benefits to sticking around. In every issue of
our newsletter you'll find

• A free e-book
• Tips from famous authors
• Discounts on spotlight titles
• Hilarious insider publishing news
• A chance to win a prize for answering a riddle

Best of all, our readers tell us, "Your newsletter is the only one I actually read." So claim your gift today, and please stay in touch!

Sincerely,

Charlotte Ashlock
Steward of the BK Website

Questions? Comments? Contact me at bkcommunity@bkpub.com.